Pleasures of Small Motions

Pleasures of Small Motions

Mastering the Mental Game of Pocket Billiards

Bob Fancher, Ph.D.

Writers Club Press
San Jose New York Lincoln Shanghai

Pleasures of Small Motions
Mastering the Mental Game of Pocket Billiards

Writers Club Press
an imprint of iUniverse.com, Inc.

For information address:
iUniverse.com, Inc.
620 North 48th Street, Suite 201
Lincoln, NE 68504-3467
www.iuniverse.com

ISBN: 0-595-12271-X

Printed in the United States of America

For Melena

Contents

Acknowledgements

My first teacher, Fran Crimi, was the first to suggest I might have something to say about the mental game in pool. Why she thought that, when I was a rank beginner, has more to do with her generosity of mind than anything I knew at the time, and I am immensely grateful.

A few years later, Andy Holoubek, of Alco Billiards, and Richard Story, editor of *The American Cueist*, got me started writing on the mental game. I am particularly appreciative of their receptiveness to my heretical ideas. Either of them could have dismissed my thinking and quashed my efforts to develop my ideas in written form. Neither did. Quite the contrary.

Rolando Aravena and John Juback, through lessons and their excellent league systems, helped me in my development as a player.

By far and away, I have learned the most from my main teacher, Bob Watson. An original and controversial character, Bob not only taught me the game, but he inspired many directions in my thinking. He helped me have the courage to think against the grain.

My intellectual friends mostly seem to think I went goofy, by starting to write about pool instead of more professionally respectable and advantageous subjects. One, though, my dear friend Charles Scott, understood and encouraged my passion for the game. I think he was the only one of my high fallutin' friends who actually saw this project as intellectually worthy.

My wife, Melena, has supported my love for the game and my efforts for this book. How many wives would be happy that their husbands considered pool part of their business and went off to the pool hall almost every morning before getting down to earning serious money?

Melena is a treasure, and the best proof I know that we sometimes receive blessings that we in no way really deserve. Thanks, Bean.

Introduction

Everyone says that playing pool is mostly mental.

But let's call a spade a spade: Most of what passes for advice on the mental game is just flat wrong.

I started playing pool seriously in middle age, after I had become a psychotherapist and writer on psychology. (My dad was a Baptist minister, and pool was not well regarded in our house when I was a kid.) Once I had gotten some sense of the mechanics of the game, I was, of course, interested in the mental dimension. Curiously, though, the available advice violates so much of what psychology knows about the mind that I could not take it seriously. Very strange. I started trying to figure the mental game out for myself. *Pleasures of Small Motions* is the result.

Conventional wisdom on the mind game seems to be a mish-mash of macho posturing, flaky metaphysics, and hodge-podge derivatives of pop psychology. At its best, the conventional wisdom on the mental game reflects rough-and-ready lessons of experience. Even at its best, it isn't very good. Lessons of experience are often wrong.

In life and in pool, experience by itself is useless. Experience by itself is just stuff that happens. Learning from experience requires an active process, and you have to know how to conduct it. We often conduct the process badly, in life and in pool.

Think of some of the things (outside of pool) that our experience seems to teach us: The sun moves across the sky, the Earth is flat, and objects in motion tend to come to rest. Every single one of those "truths" of experience is false.

Notions people have "learned" from experience tend to be hard to dislodge, because people can point at experiences that seem to confirm the belief. After all, it certainly looks as if the sun moves across the sky.

Much conventional wisdom about the mental game is about as accurate as the belief that the sun moves across the sky. Too many people claim to have "learned from experience" notions that are just plain false. That's a bad thing, because it limits one's capacity to improve.

Underline that point: "Lessons of experience" that are actually false limit our ability to improve. They close off good thinking, and they lead us to ignore all sorts of things that could help us.

To revert to our analogy: For some purposes, it did not hurt anything for people to believe that the sun moves across the sky. But believing such a thing blocked humanity from learning a lot of other important things—such as making sense of the seasons, the tides, and the weather, for instance. Furthermore, it stopped people from even thinking about all sorts of possibilities inconsistent with the sun moving across the sky. Had we not figured out how the solar system actually works, space travel would have remained inconceivable. Ditto with satellite communications.

Similarly, many of the "truths of experience" about the mental game preclude learning how minds really work in this game. That means conventional wisdom seriously limits improvement. Our understanding of the mental game is about like medieval peasants' understanding of the solar system.

Let me give you two examples.

1. Recently, I heard a very famous commentator say: "She needs to forget it's hill-hill and just play like she would on the practice table at home." You've heard advice like that a thousand times. Unfortunately, scientific research shows that people perform better under competition than at practice.

This advice is based on the common experience of people folding under competitive pressure. However, the cause is not competition, and the solution is not to forget that you are in a tense competitive situation.

In fact, learning to concentrate on the competitive situation will sharpen your game. The question is knowing how to think about competition. Teaching people to forget that they are competing will never help them learn how to think about competition.

2. The author of a book on the mental game asks a series of questions about concentration. The answer to all the questions, he says, is to concentrate on "the contact point on the object ball." Most pool instructors say the same thing. This is based on the common experience that you must have a conscious awareness of the precise point of aim to play well.

But your body has no control over the object ball; your mind can only influence what your body can control. Concentrating on something you cannot even touch means you most probably ignore what you *can* control.

Certainly you must be aware of the point of aim; but as we shall see, awareness and concentration are not the same thing. Concentrating on the object ball means you will *fail* to pay attention to most of what you need to think about to concentrate.

False beliefs, drawn from experience, bind our minds. As long as we hold to the perspective they give us, we will never see how things really are. If, however, we step back and start over, we can gain a different perspective that holds more promise. Thus, I have started this book from fundamental questions: Why are we able to play pool at all? Why do we care? How do our minds work to enable us to play, and to learn to play better? What really happens during competition?

Notice, I do not start from the question, "How do you win?" or "How do you play your best?" Until we understand the fundamentals of how we play at all, we get ourselves on the wrong track by asking those questions. We can develop tricks and rules of thumb, but those just serve to blind us to our ignorance.

You will find here explanations of why most of the "lessons of experience" seem to be true, though they are not. I do not simply say, "Forget about it." I show the sound principles that let you extract whatever small truth conventional wisdom contains, while placing it in a broader, more well-founded context. You also find here an account of how a well-functioning mind works in pool, as best I can understand it.

I do not offer any gimmicks or tricks, which seem to be the stock-in-trade of many advisors on the mental game. Most gimmicks amount to sophisticated superstitions; they give you the illusion of control, without having any real direct effect. At best, gimmicks just gerry-rig the mind. I am not interested in helping you apply bailing wire and toothpicks to hold together bad mental processes. I am interested in explicating sound, normal processes, as they apply to pool. In my nearly fifteen years as a psychotherapist, I have become convinced that gimmicks do not really work consistently, over the long haul, but developing a sound mind does. I bring that principle with me to understanding pool psychology.

This book is based on the best of recent work on neuroscience, cognitive science, and a wide variety of traditions in clinical psychology. Where work directly in sports psychology is consistent with scientific psychology and clinical wisdom, I have used it. However, I believe that basic science, and careful extrapolations from it, are the best way to understand anything. Where shibboleths and talismans of sports psychology make little scientific sense, I have left them out of this account.

Pleasures of Small Motions is the first book in what I believe will be a new wave of scientifically sound thinking about the game. I have written this book for those who want their thinking about the mental game to be derived from sound understanding of how minds work.

I am asking you to change your entire perspective: To stop believing that the sun moves across the sky and that the Earth is the center of the Universe, to begin thinking of the world in a whole new way. I believe this is the path of progress. If pool is, indeed, mostly mental, why not begin to think about the mental game in ways that make good scientific sense, that start by addressing fundamental questions?

Learning from experience requires both sound hypotheses and further testing. You should never accept any idea, including mine, simply because it "makes sense." It must be tested against additional scientific knowledge and the breadth of your further experience. I hope that as you master the principles in this book and test them in your own experience, you will find them helpful. Better yet, I hope the process of learning and testing these principles stimulates other people to develop even better, more comprehensive principles.

Bob Fancher
Austin, Texas
Spring, 2000

Chapter One

Motivation: The Pleasures of Small Motions

Pool is a game of small motions. An eighth of an inch (or less) changes everything.

Robots are good at small motions. They can be programmed to infinitesimal precision, and they can repeat the same small motion over and over, exactly. Not so with humans.

Living things have goals and purposes; dead things do not. Robots, being dead, have no purposes, no motivation. We can design a robot to do what we want, and (unless we do a bad job designing it) we need not fear that the purposes dictating the design will conflict. We can design it to exacting tolerances, fitted for the precise, limited purpose that we want it to serve. Since its tasks are determined ahead of time and limited in scope, we need give it little flexibility.

Since a robot, being dead, has neither motivations nor moods, we never have to fear that its motivations will be at cross-purposes to each other, or that some mood relevant to one task will disable it for another. We need not bother studying robot psychology; robots have none.

Humans, though, being alive, have a body that serves a host of purposes and goals, and we can change our purposes and goals from one time and place to another. Our design is full of engineering compromises, since it must serve so many purposes, many of them idiosyncratic and defined only as we go through life. Though we have some in-born purposes and goals, most concerns of most individuals depend on the specific time and place of their births, the vagaries of their peculiar experiences. The body must be exceedingly flexible, able to work within very broad tolerances.

We do not have bodies well suited to repeat small motions, reliably, over and over. Worse, since an individual's purposes are many and changeable, motivation displays no natural harmony—we are often divided within ourselves, with one concern distracting from another. Our emotions vary with our situations, with how those situations suit our overriding concerns. We often find our emotions undermining some activity we wish to do well.

Our strengths and our weakness are one and the same: Our bodies are more flexible than robots', and we have complex minds, which have moods. We can do much more than robots. But we cannot reliably repeat tiny motions, over and over, precisely.

Robots, though, do not play pool. They cannot; the most sophisticated robots we can build, with our present knowledge, cannot perform even basic visual tasks required to distinguish one ball from another and plot a line of aim, much less choose how hard to shoot, with what sort of English. Someday, no doubt, robotics will be advanced enough to produce flawless playing machines. Whether robots ever play pool, though, will depend on whether humans care to build them to do so. The robots themselves will never care.

The Instinct for Play

Many humans, though, care for pool, and the psychology of pocket billiards must start with the question, Why? To understand any activity of life, we must understand its purposes. To understand motivation, we must understand why the activity matters. Our bodies are not particularly well suited for pool, but many of us love it. Why?

Perhaps some people have only one answer: To win. That's a bad answer, for many reasons.

For one thing, "to win" doesn't explain anything. Why would winning at pool matter to anyone? No one cares about winning at breathing or falling off logs. Why is pool an activity at which anyone would bother to compete—much less an activity where we pay money to watch others compete?

More important, "to win" is a bad answer because it cannot enable you to become good at the game. You will lose far more than you win, at least until you become a top player; and you will never win when you practice, since you will not even compete then. You need some other motivation, if you are to fulfill your purpose of learning to play well.

Winning is a great thing, and surely it will be one of the motivations for any serious player. It will not help you understand the fundamental psychology of the game, though—or keep you at the table when you are not winning.

Those of us who fall in love with the game do not do so because we love to win. We fall in love with it for other reasons: The pleasures of small motions.

We "play" pool. Why do we play anything? The scientific answer is fairly simple: for fun. At first glance, play is a very strange activity. How could it contribute to survival? Why did we evolve the capacity for play? Scholars who vex themselves over the question agree that the vital purpose of play is enjoy activities crucial to our survival at times when we are not suffering any threats to our survival. *Play is the enjoyment at leisure of abilities that originated in our struggle to survive.* When our ancestors ran after buffalo, throwing rocks and swinging clubs, they were not playing; they were surviving. When we play baseball, we use the same actions for the sheer pleasure of the experience.

We play because we enjoy the experience. We evolved the capacity to play because play hones skills that matter to our survival. Our capacity to make up games has surely aided our evolution, because we bring to the struggle to survive the skills we have developed at play. Imagine two species identical in every way, except one lacks the capacity to invent and enjoy play. The species that enjoys play possesses an immense advantage when the challenges of life call upon the skills they have perfected in their games. That species would soon eradicate its earnest, hard-working rivals, for in their play they would have developed skills beyond the natural level possessed by the creatures who did not play. Humans love to play, because our ancestors who played survived and passed us their genes. We are descendants of players. The instinct for play comes with our genes.

This helps us understand why we take an interest in games that depend on skills for which our bodies are not especially well suited. The things we can do automatically are not very interesting or pleasant—where's the challenge in breathing or falling off a log? We develop competitive games around skills that matter in life, that challenge our ability. We develop them as games because we enjoy the experience.

When we play pool, we hone and enjoy our capacities for small motions. We immerse ourselves in the pleasures of precision. Think of how often we speak of "beautiful" shots. Think of the pleasure of a smooth stroke, the thrill of a cue ball dancing with exactly-executed English, the on-a-string elegance of a well-hit object ball rolling to the pocket. I would suggest that people who love the game are fascinated by the beauty of small, precise movements.

Precision matters, for our survival, and it is precisely because it does not come automatically to humans that we can play at it.

If you cast your mind back to why you first loved the game, and recapture the sheer delight of your fine motor control making the balls move around the table the way they should, you place your game squarely within a basic human instinct: Playing with skills for the sake of the experience, rather than survival. You do much more than that, though: You discover a fundamental motivation that will serve you well whenever you step to the table. You recover pleasure in the basic activity of the game.

The Value of Proper Motivation

We can understand the importance of proper motivation when we think of the hardest part of learning to play well—doing drills. If you play to win, or to "be good" at the game, drills inevitably frustrate and bore you. There is no one to beat, and drills make clear just how "not good" you really are. If you have a great deal of self-discipline, you can make yourself do them; but you will never enjoy them. They will never be play.

Our emotions—the current leading psychological theory says—serve as barometers and bellwethers: They tell us where we are, compared to where we want to be. Emotions signal "match" or "mismatch" between intention and reality. The specific emotion we feel spurs us to act in a way that (previous experience has led us to believe) may decrease a mismatch or sustain a match. If your motivation for playing pool is to win, or to be good, drills will usually give a "mismatch" reading—you will not be winning or demonstrating your prowess. Such mismatch between purpose and achievement provokes the negative emotions all of us know too well. Stay in "mismatch" for long, and your emotions say to you, "Overpower this situation" (frustration) or "This is pointless—leave" (boredom). Neither helps you learn to shoot.

Suppose, though, that you have a different motivation—one which practice, in and of itself, fulfills. Drills can then become satisfying.

Suppose you are fascinated with the beauty and precision of how small motions cause the balls to move. Suppose you thrill to the challenge to doing well something that our flexible, complex organisms find vital but difficult. If your fundamental motivation for playing (and playing well) is the sheer beauty of moving the balls with finesse and precision, drills are ideal. You become curious, rather than bored, with the motions of your stroke and the balls. Every miss tells you something, if you know how to read it. A well-executed make thrills you.

You will become a better player faster, if your motivation for playing makes doing drills satisfying. If you do not already play out of fascination with the sheer beauty of moving the balls with finesse and precision, you would do well to cultivate such an approach, if for no other reason than increasing the time you spend doing drills.

You will find, too, that cultivating the pleasure of shooting well will help you in competition. When you are five games back in a race to eleven, or fifty balls back in straight pool, nothing spoils your play as much as preoccupation with winning. Focusing on the grace and elegance of your shots, though, pushes your competitive anxiety away from the center of your awareness. Each beautiful shot becomes rewarding in itself—rather than accentuating how far you still have to go to catch up. The satisfaction from one shot feeds into your next shot, and you get into a rhythm of satisfaction. String together a lot of beautiful shots, and you win.

Pleasure and Other Motivations

Pleasure at pool can combine with many other pleasures. Surely one is the pleasure of winning. The desire to win, like the desire to play, probably originates in our evolutionary past: The strong survive; those who play best bring the benefits of play to the field of survival. The desire to win should not be disparaged; it simply cannot be the principle motivation for pursuing the game. The desire to win is one among many motivations that help us with our game.

Little of what has been written about pool until now emphasizes the importance of pleasure; almost everything places the weight on shooting "right" and winning. "There is only one way to play—the right way," we are often told. In fact, there are many correct ways to play—as many as give you pleasure.

"There is only one way to play—the right way," is an attitude held over from an earlier time. An older regime of players, who created most of the lore and instructional information, came from a very different background, with very different purposes and mental habits, than most of today's players. Habits of mind and play suited to a different demographic and sociological situation shape the advice given to people very different in thought and purpose.

A survey done a few years back showed that about ninety percent of the people who take a first pool lesson are not playing pool a year later. I believe this is, at least in part, because pool instructors still teach an archaic attitude, with no emphasis on pleasure. For most of today's players, pool is principally recreation. If it is not fun, but a set of chores and imperatives, they will not stick with it. Why should they?

When pool was dominated by hustlers and sharks, an ethos alien to today's players evolved. For one thing, pool in the Great Depression, and for several decades after, was indeed the province of blue collar males, and the best players depended on it for material sustenance. Winning is, indeed, the most important thing, when it makes the difference between having a room to sleep in and curling up in the corner of the pool hall for the night. Winning also matters, in the hierarchical jousting of a male culture. That is one well-documented trait of men in groups: We establish a hierarchy of dominance. Pool was for decades a "bachelor culture," a haven for men for whom women were not central to life. In that culture, proving your ability to play had a great deal to do with your social standing in the culture on which your life focused.

For many players of that era, pool was not play. Pool was survival, and proof of status as a man within one's social world.

Only the tiniest minority of today's players depend on pool for their livelihoods, and the game has become less blue-collar and less male-dominated. For few of us does the pool hall constitute our principal social arena. Advice drawn from the experiential lessons of an earlier time does not really suit today's players. The significance of the game differs for us. Why and how we play cannot but differ, as well.

For most of us, playing pool combines with many purposes, and we need to answer the question "Why play pool" differently from one occasion to another. Always, for most of us, pool is play, and the fundamental answer is, "The pleasures of small motions." This answer can take many different shapes, though, depending on what other purposes we mix it with on a given occasion.

With friends, we play for fun and camaraderie. The game will vary according to the friend you are playing—your friends play at different levels of skill, with different degrees of seriousness about the game and different personalities.

In your 9-ball league, perhaps, you play to test your mettle and hone your competitive skills. Each match is unique, depending on how the season has developed and your standing at the time. Too, with different competitors you have different histories and relationships. You have arch-rivals, mentors, protegés, friends, and even enemies. With each, the particular purposes you pursue will vary.

With the local hustlers, perhaps you will play to learn something or to prove something, or to take an imaginary nostalgia trip into pool's haunted past, depending on whom you play and when.

In tournaments, the situation is different again: You will probably play tournaments to win, period.

Playing alone, you may be working on your skills, distracting yourself from life's larger issues, or just having fun.

This sort of flexibility in your approach to the game has much to commend it. If you always play the same, you severely limit how much enjoyment pool can add to your life. If you play against friends the way you play against arch-rivals (or if you play against all your friends the way you play against the most competitive, skilled friend), you will soon have few friends willing to play pool with you. If you play in your league or in tournaments like you play against friends, you will never finish in the money. If, though, you learn to adapt your game to many opponents and circumstances, you can play more often, more successfully, with more enjoyment.

Such a flexible, varied approach to your pool-playing purposes has an added benefit: When one approach isn't working, others can keep you at the table. If you only play to win, and you go into a slump, you will have a hard, unpleasant time showing up at the pool hall. Psychologists have learned that people need "multiple competencies" to sustain themselves—when something in which we take pride and satisfaction becomes unavailable, we need to be able to turn to something else to motivate and sustain us.

You will gain more from the game—and improve the most—if you cultivate the pleasures of play mixed with many other motives—victory, camaraderie, mentorship, distraction from life's difficulties, and so on. Always, though, the fundamental issue is the pleasures of small motions.

Pool is play; it should always be fun. A miserable player is a miserable player. If you cultivate the pleasures of small motions, and learn to pursue them in many different contexts, you will develop into a resilient player for whom the game makes life better.

PART ONE

SHOOTING

Chapter Two

A Sense of the Game: Conscious and Unconscious Controls

References to Zen Buddhism litter commentaries on the mental game of billiards. Odd, since pool halls boast no history of spiritual exaltation, and Zen monasteries enjoy no repute as hotbeds of billiard excellence.

I would not recommend changing religions or life philosophies to improve your pool game. Yet Zen masters discovered centuries ago something that Western psychologists only now begin to appreciate: the limitations of consciousness and the power of knowledge beyond the individual will.

In Zen practice, the self (will, calculation, conscious control, and so forth) dissolves into an awareness beyond the self. According to Buddhism, the notion that individuals are ultimate, real entities is an illusion; we are only points within a larger whole. Zen practice undermines the individualistic mind set, freeing us to experience wholeness rather than self-seeking. Zen-influenced advice on shooting pool aims to "take the ego out of the shot" and "let the shot shoot itself."

Psychology research shows that the Zen masters were on the right track: Conscious control has been vastly overrated. Indeed, two decades of research shows that most information processing and motor skills take place outside of conscious control. We perceive and control many things of which we have no conscious awareness.

Your own experience tells you the same thing. Consider reflexes: You drop a glass but catch it before it hits the floor, without any conscious awareness of, or deliberate planning about, how fast it is falling, in what direction, where to move your arm or when to close your hand. All of that perceptual and motor control happens unconsciously.

Pool players know the power of unconscious information processing, though we haven't realized that we know it. We talk freely about a person having a "good sense of the game," or we complain (on a bad day) that we "cannot get a sense of the table." We talk about "finding" a rhythm. We sometimes just "see" the angles and "feel" what needs to be done. All of these common terms bear witness to the fact that much mental work takes place below the level of consciousness. Knowing what to do just occurs to us spontaneously. The unconscious delivers to conscious awareness a finished product.

The power of Zen to improve one's game probably has to do with this: It teaches you to let your unconscious processes do their work. By countering the mistaken notion that conscious control is the ultimate arbiter of play, it relaxes the choke-hold of consciousness, creating space for the unconscious to work.

Well and good. Yet every pool instructor who has drawn breath tells you to concentrate, and we never learn new skills without careful conscious control. When we are learning, we must pay close attention, consciously, to everything we do, for reasons we shall see. Whether learning or competing, we must concentrate. Yet conscious control can destroy our play. An interesting—almost Zen—paradox!

Division of Labor, Part One

Play hones skills we have developed in the struggle to survive. We have instinctive abilities, hard-wired into being human, that pool exploits. Few, if any, of those require much conscious effort. Remember what it was like when you first fell in love with the game? When, without any lessons or sophisticated knowledge, you could just "see" how to make beautiful shots? That experience called forth instinctive abilities, immersing you in their pleasure; and in this is the birth of play.

But play *hones* skills. Play is artificial—nowhere in nature are we faced with a 4 ½ foot by 9 foot table, with a uniform cloth cover, and an assortment of perfectly symmetrical spheres, which (using a carefully crafted stick) we move about the table and into pockets according to standard rules. We do not naturally possess *enough* skills to play well this artificial contrivance called "pool." Survival has never required such levels of skill, so evolution has not selected for it. In pursuing the game of pool, we need to make full use of our instinctive abilities, while also developing new skills to such a level that they *function as if* they were natural. For this, we need a proper understanding of the interplay of conscious and unconscious controls over our play.

The general role of consciousness, and its relation to unconscious information processing, is not hard to understand: Consciousness concerns itself with choices—with how things are though they might have been otherwise (like what exact items are in our immediate vicinity, and what relevance they might have for our well-being), and what we might need to do about it that is not automatically obvious. Where the "right choice" is obvious—like removing your hand from a hot surface—you do not need conscious awareness to act. Indeed, it is well documented that action starts about half a second before we are even conscious of needing to act, in such situations.

We have "wiring" to perceive, calculate, and do some things automatically; but other things have to be controlled through conscious deliberation. Some of our "automatic" wiring is original equipment—we are born with it. These are the instinctive abilities with which evolution has endowed us. Some automatic wiring results from experience—we have done a certain thing so often, or our preferences have become so well formed and habitual, that no choice need be entertained. (Think of how many times you have been driving down a road, only to be surprised that you have no memory of the last ten miles because you were "lost in thought." Though driving is not a natural skill, you have become so good at it that you had no need for conscious awareness to drive successfully.) Where our wiring is insufficient, we have to calculate consciously how to make things work. Thus, contingent situations and acquisition of new skills require conscious control.

Careful, deliberate practice lets us build new wiring to take care of contingencies we confront repeatedly. This is a well-documented fact; researchers even know something about the precise chemical processes of forming new wiring. Until the new wiring develops, though, we must control our actions consciously—precisely because we do not yet have the wiring. Just as we have to concentrate consciously to learn to type or play a musical instrument, we have to pay conscious attention to learn to shoot. Once we have consciously carried out the practice that develops new wiring, we can do those things through unconscious processes—automatically. Thus, just as a good musician rarely thinks about individual finger motions during a performance, the good pool player need not think about most details of his play.

Why should we bother honing the unconscious controls over our play? Why go through the pain of consciously, deliberately developing our skills? Everyone knows that you have to, if you are to play well. But why? Understanding the answer is not just academic: The answer will help us learn how to let conscious and unconscious controls work together in our play.

Simply put, consciousness is severely limited in how much information it can handle. The "bandwidth" of consciousness—the amount of information it can handle—is less than one one-millionth of the bandwidth of the central nervous system. By moving a task out of the realm of consciousness, we free up consciousness to do other things. This is one reason that advanced pool players see more opportunities and strategies than less advanced players—consciousness is free to think about more possibilities because it does not have to concern itself with "the basics" of how to shoot. The more knowledge you move into the "automatic" category, the freer you are to think about the options before you on the table. You literally do not have the brain power to consider all your options, if your conscious efforts have to concern themselves with how to line yourself up, move the cue, and so forth.

Developing Unconscious Controls

Pool lends itself to developing extensive unconscious controls precisely because it is artificial. You make the same movements over and over again; you face the same angles repeatedly. The rules are always the same. Basic strategies of play apply in countless situations. If you are to hone your skills to the utmost, all of this needs to become routine—automatic, controlled by brain circuitry that needs no input from consciousness, because no choices need to be made. The more knowledge that becomes unconscious, the freer you are to consider more advanced and subtle possibilities.

How do you do that? Practice, practice, practice—but deliberately, and with appropriate conscious controls.

Drills are ideal, if you do them right, for at least two unarguable psychological reasons.

First, when we shoot pool, we use intricate, extensive circuitry evolved in our brains and bodies over thousands, even millions of years. (That is why some people are simply more talented: the relevant circuits are more functional.) However, there is no innate "pool shooting" circuitry. Shooting pool calls into action many different innate circuits, like many different skilled workers called on to build a building. Each brings his skills to the job, but these skills must be coordinated to create something that did not exist before.

We have to teach the many innate neuromuscular circuits how to work together to shoot pool. We can consciously coordinate them, if we want to waste our bandwidth on such matters; or we can build new brain circuits to tell the innate circuits how to work together to shoot effectively. To build new circuits, we need to do the same thing repeatedly, to give the body the right information for building new connections. Our experience, guided by conscious control, orchestrates the innate circuits to work together at the pool table. If we repeat the experience often enough, our nervous systems builds new circuits to use in future shots. It is as if our brains say, "If you are going to keep doing this, I'm going to build some shortcuts to take care of it automatically so we don't waste so much attention on it."

(Research shows, by the way, that we learn best if we try to take on only one new skill at a time, then give our bodies time to make the changes induced by practice. If you practice a given drill for about an hour, then wait about six hours before trying anything else new, your learning is more efficient than if you give your body a lot of information about several new skills at once.)

The second reason drills are important in developing new wiring is related to the first. As we have seen, you must consciously calculate how to make your body's many circuits work together. Conscious calculation works best if you keep most conditions constant, varying only one (or a few related ones) at a time. You calculate a plan, do it, and get a result; then you do it the same way, with a minor variation, and see what result that gives you. This is how you figure out what your body needs to do to make a shot.

These two reasons fit together. To get the innate circuits to work together, we must first consciously calculate what to do, do it, then correct our motions the next time around to see if it goes better. In conscious calculation, the "mastermind," as it were, orchestrates the work of the various discrete brain and muscle circuits. Repetition is critical to find the right orchestration. The, when you have figured out what to do, you need to do it over and over under conscious control, to give your body the information to build new circuits. Eventually, the new circuits will develop and that particular kind of shot becomes "automatic." You have quite literally built new wiring into your nervous system.

To be precise, the shot becomes "ballistic." Literally, a ballistic motion is one controlled by a neuronal circuit that, once set in motion, completes its pattern as a routine. Ballistic motions require little conscious effort—trigger them and they run their course. The more conscious, deliberate work you do at drills, the less work you have to do when you need to shoot the shot in a game, and the less likely you are to mess it up. If you program yourself for a specific ballistic motion, it runs its course once you trigger it; thus, if you have built it well, it will succeed.

Whenever you are developing a new skill, you must pay conscious attention to as much of your motion as possible. How does the stick feel on this shot? If I change the stroke just so, how does that change what I feel? What I see? How the cue ball moves? Every element of the new shot must be analyzed, perceived, and remembered. Any element of the new shot to which you fail to give conscious attention is just a "wild card"—your new skill will always lack good wiring at just that point.

One of the most consistent mistakes players make in trying to learn new skills is attending to only part of the process—usually the cue ball and object ball, maybe to the velocity of the cue stick. Because our bodies have such wide ranges of motions, and because good shooting requires very small motions, this simply will not do. The precise motions needed for the shot you are trying to learn will never become part of the routine—part of the unconscious controls over that shot—unless you pay attention precisely to what each part of the motion feels like (or looks like, if it is in your line of sight) and fits with the other motions required to make the shot. Because your *natural* abilities are not sufficient to play the game to its maximum possibilities, you will never become consistent if you fail to *acquire* deliberately the exact motions required by the shot.

A good technique for assessing how well your new wiring is developing is this: Choose a new skill—maybe a particular shot, or a particular three-ball sequence that you want to run in order. Without bothering to think about it, shoot the shot (or sequence) ten times, as fast and thoughtlessly as you can without getting sloppy. Make a note of how many times you make the shot. Afterwards, work on the same skill for a solid hour, paying close attention to the sensations involved in every aspect of your play, from the tension in your legs to the feel of the cue stick to the sight of follow through to the image of the balls moving around the table. Then forget about it for the day. No more drills. Shoot racks, play a match, whatever—just don't work too hard. Over the course of a week, work consciously and deliberately on the shot—no fast or thoughtless play during this time—two or three times, for half an hour or so each time. Then come to the pool room, warm up with a couple of racks, and again shoot the shot (or sequence) ten times as fast and thoughtlessly as you can (without getting sloppy). Compare the results to the first day. Chances are you will see significant improvement.

If you do this for several weeks, you may find yourself reaching a plateau that you cannot surmount. If so, you have probably failed to analyze some element of the shot. Go back to basics: Study every move, consciously, again. Which element have you forgotten to pay attention to? Which has not become automatic?

Division of Labor, Part Two

The critical question, though, is not how to build new wiring. If you practice carefully and systematically, in the way every good instructor tells you, the new wiring takes care of itself. The more critical question is how to integrate conscious and unconscious controls when you play. Even the best players often cripple their games by trying to exert excessive conscious controls, thus undermining unconscious controls. Beginning and intermediate players do this constantly.

One of the great strengths of humans is the power of consciousness to veto unconscious processes. Our flexibility, our ability to choose, our self-discipline, our social relations, our careers—all depend on our ability to decide consciously to demur from this or that instinctive course of action. This strength, of course, can become a weakness—we can question ourselves to death, we can contort and disable our instinctive abilities, we can override the obvious and easy solution to a problem, we can make a conscious choice for which our unconscious wiring is ill-suited.

The first step in integrating conscious and unconscious controls is to *trust what you possess*. You possess both innate wiring and, more important, the wiring you have built as you have practiced. Trust it; let it do its work.

What does that mean, exactly? Consciousness, like the manager of a business, can work with or against underlings. Consciousness can be part of the team, letting everyone else (that is, unconscious processes) do what they are good at and devoting itself to its executive tasks, or it can refuse to trust the underlings, worrying to death what they have already done quite well.

When you try to control everything consciously, you ignore or veto the knowledge of your unconscious. You act like the manager who thinks no one other than himself knows anything. You destroy the work of your innate wiring and all you have learned from experience. Why did you spend all that time honing your skills, if you are not going to let them do their work? You must allow your unconscious mind to do its work and deliver the results to awareness, where you use it but must not override it.

"Use it but don't override it"—what does that mean?

Consciousness must treat the work of the unconscious as the resource that it is, rather than acting as overlord. The unconscious delivers what it knows to consciousness; consciousness feeds back to the unconscious new information; the two weave together a sense of what to do.

You must always take your "sense" of what needs to be done on a given shot very seriously. As you approach the table, just look at it, without much conscious deliberation. You will see the lay-out of the balls take on a shape—like making a picture from clouds. *This shape is not an objective fact about the table*; it is what *your* specific abilities "make" of the lay out of the balls. It is a perceptual *interpretation* of the table. The combination of your innate talents and your acquired skills have analyzed what *they* can do with exactly this situation, and the patterns you see are the result. Thus, your "sense" is very specific to you; it emerges out of what you already know. This has a distinct advantage: Your unconscious is not going to propose something it has no idea how to do. You can be sure that your "sense" of what to do (unlike some consciously calculated strategy) lies within reach of your abilities.

Most of the time, your sense of what to do leaves some questions unanswered. "All right—fine. But then how do I get onto the four ball?" This is where conscious calculation enters the discussion. "Well, maybe a little more right hand English on the three than you were thinking, and a hair more velocity?" Sit with that possibility for a moment; see how it feels. That is, wait for your unconscious processes to see whether your conscious proposal sits well with them. If not, try again. Maybe the unconscious says, "Of course—brilliant suggestion. Why didn't we think of that?" Maybe the unconscious says, "Come on—you know we are not all that precise with English on such a long shot. Can't you come up with something better?"

Never try to calculate a shot without paying close attention to the messages that come from the unconscious. That is, never proceed without—and certainly never dismiss—a "hunch." Indeed, if you cannot reach a conclusion integrating conscious and unconscious perceptions, go with your hunch. If you are an experienced player who has developed good skills, your hunch—the message from the unconscious—is likely very sound. Certainly your hunch is likely to be within the range of your ability, as your conscious decision may not.

Relaxing Conscious Controls

One way to practice relaxing your conscious controls is shooting "wing" shots. Hold your cue stick in your right hand (or left, if you are a lefty). Hold the cue ball between the thumb and index fingers of the other hand, with an object ball between your pinky and the outer edge of your hand. Position your feet for a shot; roll the object ball and set the cue ball down; shoot while the object ball is in motion. As you get the hang of this, you will find yourself making split-second decisions where and how to shoot, and you will even find yourself developing the ability for a practice stroke or two. You will be amazed at the shots you begin to pull off. That is testimony to your unconscious wiring—when shooting wing shots, you simply do not have time to override the decisions of the unconscious.

Wing shots carry a danger, though—you may just get sloppy and wail blindly at the ball. This defeats the purpose; you must shoot the shot you see, and just don't shoot if you do not see one.

Another way to practice is to throw out three balls, then shoot the sequence that first comes to mind, without bothering to ask yourself too many questions. Chances are, you will find yourself "getting shape" in ways you never would have imagined consciously.

Perhaps the best way to learn to relax conscious controls, though, is simply to play your hunches from time to time, in matches whose outcome does not matter. When you play with a friend whose skill is lower than yours, or when you are too tired to care very much about winning, or when you just want a break from worrying how well you play, do whatever occurs to you as you approach the table. Watch the outcome as an event happening in the world, as if you were a spectator, rather than as an action reflecting on your expertise.

Of course, you cannot do this unless, as the Zen types advise, you remove the ego from the shot. If winning is the only thing that matters, and winning is an ego thing for you, you will never be able to relax conscious control in a match situation sufficiently to try this. Too bad. One of the best ways to develop trust in your unconscious controls is watching, in amazement, the things that can happen when you just play your hunches.

Since consciousness attends to contingencies, and since each of us varies significantly from one night to the next, no rules can be prescribed as to just how much conscious control you will need to exert on a given occasion. Some nights we are "on" physically, and we face very few game situations beyond our automatic abilities. The whole match just seems to play itself, with minimal conscious effort. Other nights, we can't hold the stick straight without reminding ourselves.

Still, the moral of the story is to practice carefully whenever you need to develop new skills, but to relax your conscious control whenever you play. Some nights, or some shots, you need a bit more conscious effort than others. But the more knowledge you have made second nature—the more skills you have committed to unconscious control—the richer (and more accurate) your "sense" of things and the freer your consciousness to consider more advanced issues.

Chapter Three

Concentration: The Well-ordered Mind

A certain pro—best left unnamed—suffers a well-earned reputation for falling apart. Despite a top-ten ranking, many top-five finishes, and over ten years touring, this player has yet to win a pro tour tournament. If you know what to look for, you can spot the crash-and-burn moment: Posture changes, with the shoulders going slack and the body flouncing and flopping like a rag doll as the player moves around the table. This is the moment concentration vanishes.

The player would probably deny it, insisting that, in fact, concentration increases—after all, if you watch, you can see an intense effort to think through and focus on every shot. We know, though, from the ill-controlled bodily motion that concentration is gone. Concentration, contrary to popular belief, is always about the body.

Everyone knows concentration is crucial to good play. What is remarkable is how poorly most advisors on the mental game understand this critical factor. If you have the courage to ask your instructor what he means when he keeps saying, "Concentrate," most likely he will give you a bunch of phrases that seem to say the same thing (but really do not), like, "Focus! Don't let anything distract you!" Focus on what? Avoid distraction how? He will probably tell you what to think or not think about. "Don't think about the score. Don't think about the last bad shot you made. Just focus on what's in front of you." If you press, he will probably offer you some gimmick, telling you to develop a ritual or an internal command, or to focus on some specific item, like the chalk or the cue tip or the point of aim. None of that is terribly wrong, but none of it is particularly enlightening.

The word "concentration" comes from the same root as "concentric," as in "concentric circles." It simply means "with a center." To concentrate is to establish a center, around which other matters are systematically arranged. Concentration is simply centered, well-ordered thinking.

Concentration in a Nutshell

What is well-ordered thinking in shooting pool?

Let's start with a very abstract, general description: When you have a task to accomplish, the proper center for your thinking is the thing *(a)* within your control that *(b)* will determine whether you accomplish your goal. Well-ordered thinking connects the center to the goal, taking into account everything that will affect whether you attain the goal.

You organize your thinking to consider everything precisely as it impinges on whether the task succeeds. What obstacles, opportunities, obligations, tools, and sources of information can (or must) you work with? Each element involved in the task—everything that poses a choice for what to do—must be given a specific place in your thinking, appropriate to its role in fulfilling the goal. You must decide what will be done at every step of the way.

In doing so, you construct a *dynamic image* of the task. You construct, in essence, a movie in your mind, representing exactly what is going to happen. The quality of your concentration depends on the completeness of your dynamic image.

The motion of the object ball derives from the cue ball, which derives from the stick motion, which derives from your body. The center of the shot is always your body. That's the only thing you can control. Your dynamic image of the shot centers on the bodily motions necessary to make the shot.

Concentration always starts from and centers on your body—its current state when you start the shot and what it must do, if you are to complete a well-formed shot. Central to your mental organization, then, is the current state of your body, what motions it must execute to complete the shot, and how to get from here (the current bodily state) to there (the completed stroke).

Everything else—the cue stick, cue ball, object ball, lay of the table, competitive situation—constitutes *information* the mind needs if it is to guide the body. Anything that may contain information must be considered and evaluated. That is the entire and exclusive value of anything other than information about your body: to give your mind the information to tell your body what to do.

The first phase of concentration is constructing a dynamic mental image of the shot. You imagine the shot, taking place across time. However, this dynamic image must be comprehensive and precise. Your dynamic image of the shot factors in all the information provided by the lay of the balls, the motion of the cue stick, and so forth. Each element gives information on what your body must do. The information is arranged into a moving picture of what will happen as you shoot.

This image will guide what psychologists call a "feedforward process." Any kind of deliberate, purposeful action—including making a pool shot—depends on "feedforward." Feedforward consists of (*a*) a mental representation—a dynamic image—of what is going to happen, (*b*) attention to what in fact is happening as you undertake the action, (*c*) comparison of the action to the image, and (*d*) correcting the action—where need be—to conform to the image. The image guides the action.

The term "feedforward" refers to the fact that the image of what is going to happen refers forward, to the future. Fundamental to well-ordered thinking is a dynamic image adequate to guide the feedforward process.

Constructing an adequate feedforward image is only the first phase of concentration. The second phase of concentration is the feedforward process itself. In that process, you undertake the action your feedforward image portrays, and you attend to the interplay between that image and what you actually do, correcting your motions along the way by reference to your feedforward image.

Since the second phase of concentration consists of guiding your actions by comparison with your feedforward image, the image must be detailed and complete: If you do not have a representation of what is going to happen, beginning to end, at some point in the shot your body will lack guidance. At that point—no matter how carefully you focus on some other part of the shot—you will, in essence, wail blindly at the ball. Quite literally, you will have no idea what you are doing. Since pool is a game of small motions, you need only a small gap in your feedforward image, a minute moment in which your body must guess how to get from one motion to the next, to ruin your entire shot.

Perhaps the most overlooked dimension of planning a shot—and an absolutely crucial element of the feedforward image—is the *precise bodily sensations* you will have at each step of the way. Your body (obviously) can only receive information through its own sensations, so anticipating what each step of the shot will feel and look (and even sound) like is critical, if you are to be able to compare what you plan with what actually happens. Your dynamic image must include exactly what sensory experiences you expect will occur at each moment in the action, since the feedforward process depends on comparing the sensations you actually have with the ones you anticipate.

That, in a nutshell, is concentration: Constructing a complete image of the shot, centering on your body, then undertaking and guiding your bodily motions by reference to that image. "By reference to that image" means you pay attention to what you actually do, compare it to the image, and make corrections as needed.

Filling in the Picture

When we act, most bodily sensation never enters awareness. If we had to wait for conscious awareness of each sensation, and make a conscious comparison of each sensation with our feedforward image, we would lose the opportunity to act. Fortunately for us, we have evolved extensive unconscious machinery to take care of this problem.

To develop the unnatural level of skill required to play pool, however, we must train our usually-unconscious processes consciously, as we have seen. If we are to be able to concentrate to the extent necessary to play well, we must develop a rich repertoire of feedforward images through deliberate, conscious practice—then let them do their work as we play. Concentration calls into action unconscious controls we have consciously developed.

Precisely for that reason, *learning to concentrate is not a matter of learning to focus*. Quite the contrary. Learning to concentrate requires developing *unconscious* processes that function smoothly from planning the shot to follow-through. By definition, we cannot focus on unconscious processes. Learning to concentrate requires developing skills on which you will rarely focus.

You absolutely must develop keen body awareness when you practice, if your concentration is ever to be well developed. This seems unnatural—we want to pay attention to the object ball or the cue stick, not to our own bodies. It *is* unnatural, in the sense we have already explained: Play hones skills beyond their natural states. You must deliberately, consciously, systematically develop an accurate sense of the bodily sensations involved in executing your shots correctly. You will not, once you have done this, routinely focus on such sensations. They will, however, always be the center of your shooting. Without this, your feedforward process, and thus your concentration, will always be faulty.

So how, exactly, do you concentrate?

When you are learning to concentrate, as with any new skill, you need to control your thinking deliberately. You need to make a conscious effort to think through the entire picture of the shot. What must that picture include?

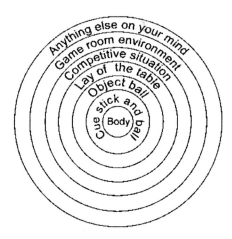

The metaphor of concentric circles helps. We can imagine "seven circles of concentration." At the center is always your body—each of the other "circles of attention," we may call them, refers back to the body. *Your feedforward image is complete only if it includes the bodily sensations each outer circle implies—you must know the sensations to expect in relation to the cue ball, the cue stick, the point of aim, and so forth.*

What will your stance feel like? The tension in your hand as you hold the stick? The angle of your wrist? The motion of your arm? What will the cue stick look like as it moves through the stroke? What will you see as you eye the point of aim? As the cue ball travels its line? As the cue ball and object ball make contact? As the object ball travels toward the pocket and the cue ball moves around the table?

Every element of the shooting situation gives your body instructions. Even the image of how the balls will move around the table *after* you have made the stroke—which might seem quite beyond your body—gives you crucial information: this image calls forth your memories of how much force and English to use to make the balls move just exactly that way—and precisely what it *feels like* to do exactly that. The image of the cue stick following through the cue ball, likewise, guides your motions: With your actions aiming to make the stick move smoothly to the follow through point, you control the stick more effectively before it ever gets there. (Every beginning player thinks follow-through is irrelevant, and almost no one explains why that is an error. Well, when do you think the stick goes out of control, to end up akilter after contacting the cue ball? Do you think you control the stick beautifully, until the point of contact, then lose control of it? Hardly. Follow-through is important because getting from the start of the stroke to the proper follow-through position controls the stick all the way through the stroke.)

Some advisors would have you believe you should pay no attention to the competitive situation or the game room environment; but that is just silly. You will, in fact, pay attention to the competitive situation—are you back three games early in a race to eleven, or late? Ahead and on a roll? Is there money on the match? We are human, not robots; the competitive situation affects our concerns, hence our actions. The only question is whether you will think about these things deliberately and decide exactly what they mean for your shot, or whether you will let them kick around, unaddressed, as disrupters of your play. (Just how you should think about them, we will address in a later chapter.)

Even the game room environment is relevant: What, if anything, is going on that you need to take into account? Anyone who waits to shoot until some distracting motion has ended demonstrates that a good player notices what is happening in the room and factors it in.

While you are assessing and planning, let your attention bounce back and forth from one circle to another—play with the possibilities of how each might be experienced, if you shoot one way rather than another. Let your unconscious knowledge make its contribution—pay attention, consciously, to the hunches your unconscious processing provides, and play with them, along with all the other possibilities you imagine. Let an image of the shot take shape.

What matters is not some ritualized method of thought, but letting yourself create a complete feedforward image. While you are learning to concentrate, double check the image as it emerges. Have you failed to consider anything? Do you lack an anticipatory sensation of some point in the process?

Using information from the "seven circles," create a movie in your mind; imagine how all the elements will combine, imagine the sequence of every motion and sensation from approach to follow-through. Only when you have developed this dynamic image are you ready to shoot.

When you have a sense of how the whole shot is going to go, start your shot. As you drop down over the table, notice the sensations you are having and check them against your dynamic image. Eye the cue ball, move the stick toward it in your practice stroke, eye the object ball, etc.—always comparing the sensations to the feedforward image. Where your sensations differ from what you expected, correct your motions—or get up and start over. Always, the sensations of the shooting motion and the feedforward image intertwine dynamically, as you check the real process of shooting against the feedforward image. Always, awareness of your body must be central as you shoot.

This process will feel awkward as you practice it—you are literally trying to focus consciously on what is usually unconscious (and will be again). As you become adept at attending to every element of constructing a feedforward image and attending to it as you shoot, you will need to pay progressively less conscious attention to the process.

When you have mastered the process of concentration, it usually flows easily, and you will no longer have to remind yourself of the different steps—just as you do not have to check your bridge, stance, and so forth once you have learned them and you are playing fluidly. As with all pool knowledge, learning makes it automatic, and you will need to make a deliberate effort only when something is wrong.

Focus

What, then, of the usual advice to focus? Mostly, it is simply wrong, in two ways: For one thing, concentration is not the same thing as focus; you may learn to focus, while failing to pay attention to most of what concentration should deal with. For another, focus does not follow any set rules. You simply should not always focus on the same thing. Focus shifts, within each shot, and from one shot to another.

Concentration embraces the whole of your thinking, including unconscious controls and the elements of consciousness outside your focus. Focus is part of consciousness, and only a part. We know that consciousness consists of "figure," which is the object of focus, and "ground," which is most of the contents of consciousness. Even within consciousness, focus is only a small part of your mental activity. If you think focus is the essence of concentration, you will usually leave most of what you need to think about unattended. You will pay attention to only part of consciousness, leaving all of the rest of your mental organization—which is most of your mental activity—to chance. You will fail to master most of the mental organization essential to concentration. You will lack the breadth of mental control to play well.

Not only is focus just a part of the mind; you should not always focus on the same thing. Focus will vary from situation to situation, depending on which information you can successfully process without bothering to be conscious. Focus is always relative to what you know—that is, what is automatic for you and what requires more conscious control—what situation you face, and how you are playing at the specific time. There can be no set rules always to focus on a certain thing.

Rules always to focus on the same thing try to make consciousness something it is not—namely, a constant. But consciousness, as we have seen, concerns itself with contingencies and choices. Contingencies, by definition, cannot be predicted. You cannot know in advance what choices you will face, or what must be considered to make and execute what you choose. If you are an advanced player, having a good night, you will pay little conscious attention to your body or the mechanics of shooting—those are so routine for you that you have relatively few choices to make. Some shots will require attention to the angle of the stick, perhaps, when you are jacked up behind a ball, or careful focus on the point of aim, when you've left the cue ball too close to the object ball. Mostly, though, you will focus on strategy or rhythm or the smooth, wonderful feeling of how well you are playing.

Most of us have few of those nights—and even the best pros have more nights of hard choices than magical perfection. The less advanced our abilities—the less that is automatic for us—or the worse night we are having, the more attention we have to pay to bodily sensations or the mechanics of shooting.

Focus is simply the center of consciousness. No one can tell in advance what it should be on a particular shot, other than this: You should focus on whatever requires the most conscious attention at the moment of shooting. If you always focus on the same thing, you have defeated the purpose of conscious attention. You have made consciousness a constant, not the executive in charge of contingencies. You have made yourself mentally rigid and guaranteed that much of the time you will be focusing on the wrong thing.

Perhaps most instructors forget that you perceive many things consciously besides the center of your attention. (Psychologists say you can be aware of seven items of information, plus or minus two, at a time.) Perhaps their rules about what you should "always" focus on tell us, correctly, that we must always be conscious of certain things. You will, of course, always have a conscious perception of the point of aim, for instance—but it need not be your focus. You may, on a given occasion, focus on the sensations involved in moving the cue stick or maintaining a balanced stance or hitting the cue ball in just the right spot, even as your conscious awareness of the point of aim works just fine.

You have to know what you are good at; you have to know what you have and have not mastered. You have to know how well you are playing, how challenging a particular shot will be for you under the circumstances you face. You have to know what requires the most conscious attention on the specific shot before you, on this specific occasion. Since occasions vary in what they require of consciousness, if you always focus on the same thing, you will often focus on the wrong thing.

Understanding what constitutes proper concentration can help you choose focus, however. You can run through a checklist of what constitutes a complete feedforward image and see whether you have each element under control, then focus wherever you fall short.

Something you will never learn, if you confuse focus and concentration, is that the better you are, the less conscious effort you have to expend to achieve concentration. The more skills you commit to the realm of the automatic, and the more you cultivate good habits of mental organization, the less attention you must pay to achieve concentration. Your habits of concentration themselves become automatic.

You acquire habits of concentration by practicing them, as I have explained them to you here, not by having to reinvent your good mental organization through conscious effort every time you step to the table. The better you are, the less conscious effort you will usually put into achieving concentration—your consciousness becomes free to pay more attention to advanced possibilities, less attention to such basics as the point of aim, because all the basics are under unconscious control. For the best players, playing at their best, focus has next to nothing to do with concentration. Their excellent automatic abilities give them concentration unconsciously, and consciousness is free to consider the most advanced contingencies.

The worst thing you can do in cultivating good mental habits is to forget the entire concentration process and just focus on some predetermined facet of shooting. If you focus without attending to the broader tasks of concentration—like the pro who falls apart—you will almost always ignore most of what you need to think about. Confuse concentration with focus, and you will lack both the breadth of mental order and the flexibility of mind to play well.

Distraction

And the advice to avoid distraction? What are we to make of that?

In one sense, we obviously want to avoid distraction: We want to avoid disorderly thinking, disorganized play. Yet in two senses, the usual advice about avoiding distraction is bad advice. First, the usual advice is "Don't think about" this, or that, or the other—the score, the competitive situation, the difficulty of your situation, the joy of being so far ahead, whatever. "Don't think about" is just bad advice. Anything that captures your attention requires your attention. We are creatures whose neurology evolved to alert us to things relevant to our concerns; we cannot unhook this wiring just to play pool. If something captures your attention, you need to address it—if only to decide it actually pertains to no current need.

Generally speaking, your mental machinery will not bother to alert you to things that can be taken care of automatically. You become conscious of contingencies that require decisions. If an idea occurs to you, your mental mechanism has sent you a message, "This requires your attention—we don't know what to do." If you put the idea out of your mind, you are like a (bad) manager who just ignores his underlings' bewilderment and leaves the issue for them to hash out, unguided.

Consider the ubiquitous notion that you should "put negative thoughts out of your mind." In fact, if a negative thought occurs to you, you have to deal with it. Ignoring it will not make the concern that prompted it go away. (Chapter Five explains this in detail.) In fact, if you take negative thoughts seriously and think them through, you can use them to focus and steady your play.

Consider some examples:

Suppose you are down 6-2 in a race to eleven. You think, "Oh, man—I'm in deep trouble. He only has to win five before I win nine." The correct response to such thoughts would be something like this: "That's true—no doubt about it. However, he won six out of the first eight; you could win six of the next eight. You need to settle down and choose each shot wisely, then stay carefully centered on your body. Don't go getting panicky."

Suppose you have just missed a fairly easy shot and left your opponent an easy run out—for the third time tonight. "What an idiot—am I just trying to lose this thing? What is wrong with me? I deserve to lose this one." You could dismiss such concerns, or you could take them seriously. "It's true—if he concentrates and plays well, and I don't, he deserves to win, not I. Really, what is going on with me? Am I getting too cocky? Is my mind somewhere else? Why?" Take time to answer your own questions. If, in fact, your mind is somewhere else, you need to know where and why. Deal with whatever is calling you away from good play.

Suppose you are down 8-6, and your opponent misses the seven ball—but leaves it at the head spot, with the cue ball on the bottom rail. "Oh, I can't believe this—I finally get a break, and this is the break I get? This is a really low percentage shot. I miss this, he runs out, and its 9-6." All of that is true. You have two correct options here. First, you say to yourself, "Right. This is not a great break. Don't pretend it is. Maybe I can make something of it, maybe not. What's the highest per-centage play here? Just play that one and take the consequences." Second, you might say, "This is not a great opportunity to win. Still, I have about a 20% chance of pulling off a winner with this shot. All right—that's what I'll try. I know it's a big risk, but that's my choice." Then you focus on the shot, try it—and if you miss, you just say, "Well, I shot it as well as I can. No guts, no glory."

The worst thing you can do in this situation, psychologically, is say, "Think positive. A great shot pulls this to 8-7. Forget the negatives." Why is this so bad? You are banking on a low percentage possibility, so the probability is that you will end up disappointed and angry with yourself. Would you sell your car to buy lottery tickets? It is irrational to invest your hopes in the highly improbable.

Sometimes the truth in your negative thoughts has to be teased out of excessive pessimism; but even here, you need to face the truth and decide a constructive response. Suppose that you realize you are simply overmatched—your opponent is much better than you. "I might as well go home. I have no chance against this guy." The element of truth is this: You have only a slim chance of winning. The constructive response might be to create a conservative strategy, look for weaknesses you might exploit, and get fascinated by the challenge. The worst case is that you will lose a match that, by rights, you ought to lose. Where's the shame in that? If you pay attention and rise to the challenge, this is an opportunity to test yourself and learn something—not the time to go home.

In general, negative thoughts contain information you need to take seriously. You can use this information to steady yourself, by thinking, "That's true—which is all the more reason to settle down, take my time, and concentrate."

The idea that you don't need a lot of negative thoughts distracting you from your play is correct, but the idea that putting such thoughts out of your mind helps anything is just wrong. You deal with negative thoughts by addressing them. A question answered is a question laid to rest. A question ignored is a constant irritant.

If you understand that concentration is well-ordered thinking, you can think about anything of concern without disrupting your play. The issue is not to ignore certain kinds of thoughts; the issue is to put them where they belong in relation to shooting. A negative thought can improve your play, if you use it to motivate yourself to get your dynamic image of the shot in order and carry it out smoothly. A negative thought only disrupts play if you decide that, in fact, there is no point bothering to shoot well, or if you are so busy with the negative thought that you do not bother to get your mind in good order. The problem there, though, is not the negative thought. The problem is that you do not get your mind in order.

A second, more interesting fact about distraction is this: Sometimes it helps. Indeed, some of the most common advice about concentration probably works precisely because it distracts us.

Our brains seem to have very distinct systems for handling verbal information and sensory information. While the two relate to each other in many ways, some tasks are best executed under sensory rather than verbal guidance. Pool is like that—which is why many of the best players are bad teachers: They cannot put into words, hence cannot convey to others, what goes on when they shoot. A feedforward image in pool is not a verbal matter, but a visual and kinesthetic one. Yet many of us, especially under pressure, are likely to try to think our way through the shot verbally. "Okay, now do this, and then this." This is dangerous: verbal thinking, unlike sensory representations, has no intrinsic tie to bodily motion (you can talk a good game without the skills to play one), and preoccupation with words can cause us to lose track of the bodily intelligence crucial to concentration. (One very good study of riflery competitors shows that, prior to shooting, activity in the verbal processing centers of the brain decline radically. Pool players should note that the processing of spatial relations—of special importance to us—takes place in a completely different part of the brain than verbal processing.)

If you can distract your verbal awareness, so that it does not interfere with visual or tactile awareness, you may enable your sensory and unconscious controls to work more smoothly. Most "personal commands" or "self talk" probably work to keep our verbal processes occupied while other processes control our shots. By occupying your consciousness with an undemanding, simple set of words, you prevent yourself from putting your energy into verbal thoughts that consume attention and disrupt the (sensory-dominated) feedforward process.

What kinds of distractions should we avoid, then? Anything (including bad pool advice) that disrupts concentration—anything, that is, that prevents a well-formed feedforward process centered on the body. Yet here, again, there are no rules. How many times have you seen a guy begin to shoot better when a beautiful woman starts playing at the next table? How many times have you seen a guy completely lose concentration when a beautiful woman starts playing at the next table? One person's distraction may be another's motivation. There are no rules of what you should pay no attention to, because *distraction is not an objective thing; distraction is a way of thinking—thinking in a badly ordered manner.*

How do we avoid distraction? Well, how do you avoid falling off a log? By doing a good job of walking across it. You avoid distraction by doing a good job of concentrating. If you occupy yourself with constructing a complete feedforward image, and you do not begin to shoot until you have it; and if you attend to the sensations of shooting, comparing them to the feedforward image—then you simply will not be distracted. You may take longer than necessary to construct your feedforward image, if you go off on tangents before you settle on it. You may take longer to shoot, if you have to correct for all sorts of things alien to the bodily sensations at the center of the feedforward image. As long as you know what constitutes good concentration, though, and you do whatever you need on a given shot to get there, you can think about whatever you want along the way.

Concentration as Choreography

When you concentrate fully, you come close to achieving the Zen state of dissolving the self. Your unconscious processes move through consciousness without constriction, melding with the table, the room, the game itself. Consciousness is but one part of the process, and by no means the ruler. You feel one with the process, part of the flow; you seem to transcend the egocentric concerns of everyday life. Play itself, not your ego, is the thing.

Concentration is not just a means to play better. If your concentration is well formed, your experience of shooting will have the coherence and completeness of a good story or a beautiful song. Your bodily motions will be fluid, choreographed by the feedforward image. Guided by a well-ordered mind, play achieves sensual and pragmatic unity and completeness. The pleasures of play, organized through the well-ordered mind, become more than random, inchoate moments of satisfaction. They unite into something very like a work of art.

Chapter Four

Rhythm: Put Some Music in Your Moves

A friend of mine teaches elementary school music, and for his wedding, he had a group of his students perform. Bad idea. Cute, but bad. Since my friend was busy getting married, the students played without a director. No one kept a beat, and the songs were completely unrecognizable. With every student playing a different rhythm, or no rhythm at all, chaos ensued.

Pool players talk about "finding a rhythm." However, we tend to talk about rhythm as a mysterious effluvium we enter more or less by accident. We "find" it. No one says how—or even why it matters.

Why it matters is simple: Rhythm is how the band plays together.

Why Rhythm Matters

Neuroscientists have discovered that people are "modular"—that is, our bodies and brains consist of many different "modules," each with specific tasks, that work in parallel (that's techno-speak for "at the same time") to perform complex tasks. Think of several hundred (or thousand) computers in a network, each of which is connected to a number of robots of different sorts—and think about all of those computers having to be synchronized, so that all of them work together on a problem, which requires moving the robots back and forth in a coordinated manner to get a job done. That's a good metaphor for the modules of your brain and body.

Executing a pool shot, then, requires that many different physical and mental systems work together. The activities of these many modules have to be coordinated, if the complex task is to be performed.

Moreover, complex tasks, like executing a pool shot, take place over a period of time, if only a few seconds. Not only do the many modules have to be coordinated with each other, but they have to be coordinated across a span of time.

The situation, in fact, is more complicated than that! There are time lags between sensory input, modular processing, and consciousness. The sensory signal has to pass from your finger or eye or wrist or leg—whatever—to the various modules that need the information. Thus, each module gets information that is a few milliseconds old, which it works on and passes to other modules, and so forth. The output from all of these modules has to be integrated as your brain creates a unified image for consciousness. Time passes all the while. Consciousness is always a bit behind; it is never really perception of "right now" but a prediction of what is probably going on, given what was going on half a second ago.

The situation when you are shooting, then, is this: Many different modules have distinct tasks to perform; many of those tasks have to take place at the same time, others in sequence. Except for the most primitive sensory receptors, each module does its thing with "old" information—information about stance, body tension, hand and arm motion, stick position and motion, ball position and pocket position relative to your current stance, and so forth. The various modules feed instructions to other modules that will control your motions as you shoot. Modules, most unconscious, pass information back and forth. When you "pull the trigger" the conscious sense of what you are doing relies on information about a half second old, highly processed by all your mental and physical modules. Your conscious sense may "feel right"—but it *is* right only if all the information processing was completed in good, orderly fashion.

That's why you need a good rhythm: To coordinate all the modules as they do their work through time. Rhythm is the way that every module can predict when its output will be needed, and what each other module will be doing at that instant. Rhythm is the method of coordination and prediction.

Think of someone you know who lacks a sense of musical rhythm. If you watch them try to dance (or even sway to the rhythm), you see erratic motion—sometimes they are ahead of the beat, sometimes behind, with no real pattern. Unable to anticipate the beat, they try to guess when it will be, and they get it wrong. Then watch someone with a good sense of rhythm. He (or she) starts all parts of the body moving at just exactly the right amount of time before the beat, so that the dance motion is complete on the beat. The beat organizes his motions, so that he is fluid and coordinated, and everything happens together right on time. Even so with a pool stroke: Rhythm organizes and coordinates the motion.

Rhythm controls and coordinates the various bodily processes, over time, so that everything gets done harmoniously and in good order. The key point is that *rhythm controls*. That is, you must let the rhythm rule your motion. Otherwise, your stroke is like the little orchestra at my friend's wedding—all over the place, with no discernible order.

Rhythm ties together everything we have learned so far in this book. Rhythm is the timing device that lets the unconscious and conscious controls over your play work together, that moves the "movie in your head" forward as you go from imagination to execution. Rhythm is the physical medium that transforms concentration into action. Rhythm is the mind/body connection in your play. Rhythm, then, is absolutely fundamental to good play.

Because rhythm is so important, the idea of "finding" your rhythm is, in a sense, a dangerous notion. The problem? When we think of rhythm as something that we "find," we think of it as a hit-or-miss thing, something we may or may not stumble into. Why leave to chance whether you happen across this central axis of excellence?

Rhythm, like everything else in pool, involves two principles we have emphasized many times: When you practice, you can consciously develop mechanisms that can function without deliberate control when you play, and the best play builds on natural skills deliberately honed beyond their natural level.

Understanding Rhythm

Rhythm has two dimensions: Cadence (the "beat") and tempo. Cadence is cyclical and provides the structure of the rhythm. That is, the cadence consists of structured cycles, which repeat one after another—like the cadence of a march. The tempo provides the motion. Tempo consists of how many cycles of your cadence you execute in a given span of time—so, for instance, you can play at a rate of, say, six cycles per minute, or thirty. The latter is five times as fast, but it has exactly the same structure.

Tempo varies significantly—we will discuss that a few pages from here—but cadence need not. Cadence lends itself more easily to deliberate development. You can develop a cadence that fits your style of play, then rely on it all the time.

Music and dance provide the clearest examples of rhythm. All of us (at least, all of us who can keep time to the music when we dance, sing, or tap our feet) know some basics about cadence. We know, for instance that a four-beat cycle goes 1-2-3-4, 1-2-3-4, with the emphasis on "1" and a weaker emphasis on "3." (Think of "Ninety-nine bottles of beer on the wall"). A three-beat cycle goes 1-2-3, 1-2-3, like a waltz. Our natural sense of rhythm provides the starting point for a deliberate understanding of playing with rhythm. If you think about it, you will realize that rhythmic play, like music, has a clear cadence. Watch a player who is "in stroke," and you can count it out like a dance.

While music and dance provide the most obvious examples of rhythm, rhythm is pervasive. You probably don't realize it, but one of the differences between good writing and bad, good movies and bad, or a compelling speech and one that puts you to sleep, is rhythm. An expert book designer will choose a font and a format that "match" a writer's rhythm, so that the visual rhythm and the rhythm of the prose complement each other. Similarly, a competent pool player, when he is "on" his regular game, has a rhythm, even if it is no more obvious than the rhythm of good acting in a movie or good writing in a book.

Rhythm does not mean mechanical repetition of motions; it means that motion, however varied in its content and direction, follows an underlying cadence, at a discernible speed. A garden-variety dancer doing a simple waltz repeats the same motions over and over; but a world-class ballroom dancer, using exactly the same music, waltzes in a fluid and dramatic manner that involves little obvious repetition. Underlying both the simple and the sophisticated waltzes, though, is exactly the same cadence. The world-class dancer, no less than the stumbling beginner, is counting under her breath, 1-2-3-, 1-2-3, 1-2-3.

Arrhythmia—failure of rhythm—is the most common bad habit in all of pool. Even many pros suffer it. This is because pool players do not learn deliberately about rhythm from the time we begin to play. We know the value of rhythm, once we have become proficient enough in the basics to "find" a rhythm from time to time. However, we do not know how to find it, and we do not make developing it a priority. Thus, by the time we think about it, we have developed a host of habits that undermine optimal rhythm. Even good players tend to be sloppy about rhythm.

In the best of all possible worlds, you would learn to pay attention to rhythm from your earliest lessons. You would realize that your rhythm is as important as your bridge, and you would develop your rhythm as you developed your stroke. That is not the world in which we live.

Most pool players are like mediocre dancers, who possess a natural sense of rhythm but never develop any precision. Like bad or inexperienced dancers, they are so worried about whether they are going to make the next step work just right that they miss the beat. They wobble around their proper rhythm, sometimes falling into it and playing beautifully, but often not.

Like insecure dancers, or dancers learning a new routine, most pool players incorporate an excess of conscious controls and deliberate checks that make a smooth rhythm nearly impossible. They pay so much attention to consciously controlling the sequence of motions that they lose track of the beat. Good dancers know to let the rhythm organize their motions. They know to relax their conscious controls once they have memorized the sequence. They know to let the rhythm become paramount. Pool players, though, often build into their strokes the stuttering, halting, arrhythmic awkwardness of first learning a dance. They never become fluid, but instead—without realizing it—pride themselves on their lack of rhythm, calling it "concentration."

The effort to coordinate your motions through conscious controls, rather than by rhythm, destroys your play, for two reasons. First, most of the many different modules that have to work "in parallel" cannot be consciously controlled and coordinated. Furthermore, consciousness by itself is always behind, so efforts at conscious control disrupt processes dependent on modules that do their work "earlier" in the sequence.

You already know a great deal about shooting. You already have something of a stroke and style of your own. Your style is built around some basic rhythm, but you have not paid attention to developing and disciplining it. Chances are quite high that your style is riddled with arrhythmic elements impeding the smooth flow of your natural rhythm.

In other words, your style of play contains the seeds of a steady cadence, covered over with bad habits. If you want to play your best, you simply must do the work to remove the bad habits and hone your rhythm beyond an instinctive level. You have to ferret out the underlying cadence, then discipline your play to conform to it consistently. You have clean up your play to "dance" to that rhythm all the time.

Becoming Rhythmic

If you have a well-developed style of play, the beats per cycle (cadence) of your rhythm should usually be the same, all the time. The cadence of your stroke, like the cadence of a specific dance or a particular tune, is always itself. Your cadence is intrinsic to your stroke.

Notice, though, the term "well-structured style of play": A well-developed stroke lends itself to a well-structured cadence; a chaotic, disorderly stroke does not. To have a good rhythm consistently, you simply must develop a disciplined, well-structured stroke. If you do not, you will never attain a consistent rhythm. You will always be *looking for* your rhythm rather than simply *knowing* it.

You can develop—not just "find"—your basic cadence deliberately, in practice. You start with an analysis of the stroke. Everyone's stroke involves two basic motions—back and forth. Your eyes move back and forth; your stick moves back and forth. Every good rhythm will divide into some two-beat structure. All of your motions, including eye motions and the rhythm of your thinking, must fit within and be governed by a basic two-beat structure.

That does not tell us much; your stroke may require a two-beat structure over a four beat cadence—like a strong beat on one and a weak beat on three (1-2-3-4)—or even over a six-beat structure (1-2-3-4-5-6). Or your cadence may require the two organizing beats to fit into a slow four-beat cadence (1-and-2-and-3-and-4-and).

You start your development, then, knowing that your stroke will have some sort of two-beat structure. How do you refine your cadence, though? How do you know whether your cadence is 1-2-3-4, or maybe 1-and-2-and-3-and-4-and, or maybe 1-ee-and-a- 2-ee-and-a, or maybe 1-and-a-2-and-a, or maybe even a plain old 1-2, 1-2?

Break your stroke down into "motions and moments." "Motions" are simply what the term says, movements. Consider your practice strokes, your eye motions, head motions, and the motions you make in assuming (and adjusting) your stance. "Moments" are times when you are not moving, but thinking, looking, checking your stance or grip, and the like. What kinds of motions, and how many of them, do you usually go through.? In what order? What kinds of moments, how many—and where do they fall in the process of stroking?

Consider how long each motion or moment tends to take. Rule of thumb: Find one element of your stroke which is already fairly consistent and take it as your starting point for a beat. For instance, your first practice stroke might always be the same, or your last stroke—from the moment you begin your back stroke until the moment of contact with the cue ball—might be your most consistent element. Your most consistent rhythmic element should be initially assumed to be one beat.

Figure out how all the other motions relate to this most consistent motion. Everything else has to be some multiple or division of that. That is, your other motions must take place at the same rate, or at a rate that is systematically related to it. Are you one of those people whose practice strokes are twice as fast as his actual stroke? Half as fast? The same? Do your moments of checking your aim match the time span of a practice stroke, half it, or double it? Or triple it? Distinguish exactly how long each of your motions takes, in relation to your basic beat. That tells you how many beats, or what fraction of a beat, each requires.

Consider which things happen at the same time. While you are finding your point of aim, for instance, what else are you doing? While you are moving your cue stick back in a practice stroke, what are your eyes doing? How many beats, or what fraction of a beat, does each motion take? Which things take place on the same beat, which ones span several fractions of a beat while others take place across those fractions? Are you, for instance, checking your point of aim across one beat, during which you make two practice strokes of half a beat each?

Videotaping your play can help you map your motions and moments. You will probably find it easier to analyze your stroke on tape, just because you are not trying to shoot and dissect your shooting at the same time. Watch the tape as if you were watching a dance; try counting different cadences, to see which ones fit most closely.

Thus, the strategy is (a) to break down your stroke into motions and moments, (b) determine the basic beat by finding your most consistent rhythmic element, (c) determine which motions and moments happen together or sequentially. As a result, you (d) sketch out how the various motions and moments correlate, so that you create a sense of "orchestration"—what has to happen, when, and in what patterns.

You will find (if you are a competent player at all) that your stroke comes close to a steady rhythm already. You will find that you tend to do things in a certain order, for certain amounts of time relative to each other, and those amounts of time tend to organize into discernible cycles. The better-developed the routines you already have, the easier to see the innate rhythm; but most of us already come within striking distance of some steady cadence.

Chances are, though, that you will find yourself to be fairly amateurish, from a rhythmic perspective. That is, you will be like the amateur musician who basically keeps the beat, but sometimes throws in extra half-measures, or who gets behind the beat a little one minute then rushes ahead the next. You will be able to see what the cadence wants to be, what cadence your body is trying to follow; but you will also see that you are none too precise in fulfilling it.

If this innate cadence makes itself clear, clean it up. As you practice, count out the cadence and make yourself follow it, however strange that feels. At first, you will find this difficult: You will feel insecure, wanting to interject conscious checks and controls that disturb the flow of the rhythm. Well, don't.

If you will count the cadence deliberately, and make yourself follow it, you will be shocked to find yourself start to make shots more consistently. The reason is simple: Your coordination (including hand/eye coordination) will begin functioning better. You will stop undermining the natural, rhythmic coordination of your many physical and mental modules.

Add a rhythm drill to your practice: For ten or fifteen minutes, set up one simple shot, over and over again. Count out your cadence as you shoot it, and make *following the cadence* the *only* objective. Start with a simple center-ball shot. As you are learning to clean up and discipline your rhythm, do this every day. Once you have gotten comfortable doing the drill with center-ball, you can do it using a more sophisticated shot—draw or follow, high right or low-left, whatever. However, only do the drill with one sort of shot at a time: Do it only with draw one day, only with follow another, and so forth.

You will probably be surprised to find this difficult. You will probably find yourself "stuttering," pausing at various points—especially just before the last stroke—and disrupting the rhythm to insert a conscious check. That is precisely the sort of thing you want to eliminate. The idea is to get comfortable letting your rhythm organize your shot, with your conscious calculations becoming just part of the process. Your conscious checks have to take place *within* the rhythm, and the rhythm, not conscious decisions, must determine when the cue stick strikes the cue ball.

Once your cleaned-up-and-disciplined rhythm has become second nature, you can drop this drill—but pick it up again when you find yourself in a slump.

Having discovered your cadence and disciplined your play to follow it, you can count it out to yourself like a drill team captain whenever you need. You won't always have to—once you have developed it, generally it will just come naturally. But when you are off, you can count it out deliberately to get in rhythm.

Of course, if you cannot analyze your stroke into a well-ordered, regular pattern, you have some work to do! Unless you have a regular, dependable pattern to your stroke, the many modules required to execute it never know just how to coordinate themselves, and you will be extremely inconsistent in your play. (Sound familiar?) If you are always trying to "find" a rhythm, instead of playing the rhythm that fits your stroke, chances are that you simply lack a well-structured stroke.

If the innate cadence is not fairly clear, you have to start more or less from scratch to figure out how your motions and moments can hang together in a rhythmic sequence. You must rebuild your stroke from the ground up, to deliberately cultivate a structured stroke. (In my teaching of beginning students, I do this beginning in the second lesson.) Pretend you know nothing more than the basic mechanics of making a stroke.

Approach the table counting rhythmically, 1-2-3-4, 1-2-3-4. Stand two steps from the shooting position, counting under your breath all the while. Find the point of aim on the object ball. Plan your shot. Construct your feedforward image. Count all the while. Then step forward on 1, move your back foot into position on 2, drop (keeping your eye on the point of aim on the object ball) on 3 and 4. Move the cue stick forward toward the cue ball on 1, as your eyes drop to find the point at which you intend to hit the ball. On 2, start your backstroke, as your eyes go up to the point of aim on the cue ball. On 3, move the cue back toward the cue ball, while again dropping your eyes to the cue ball. On 4, move the cue back, as you again lift your eyes toward the object ball. Keep your eyes on the ball, and shoot precisely *on* 1—then hold your position as you count out "2-3-4."

Keep the cadence steady, and keep your motions in time to this cadence. Eliminate "stuttering"—breaking your rhythm to make conscious checks. Eliminate nervous, arrhythmic motions, like juggling the cue stick before or between your practice shots. Discipline every motion to take place precisely in time with the cadence.

Once you have mastered this very simple structure, you can start trying variations. Add extra practice strokes. Try making your practice strokes half as fast as your final stroke, or twice as fast. But be deliberate in your experimentation. If you are not deliberate as you experiment, something may work—and you won't remember exactly how you did it, or whether it works better than something else. If you are deliberate, though, and modify your cadence thoughtfully, you will develop a style and cadence that suits you.

A structured stroke, with a constant cadence, does not mean that you have to make exactly the same motions, mechanically, every shot. It does mean, though, that variations follow the pattern. You can interject extra practice strokes, or extra moments of rest as you check your aim or balance, as situations demand it. But you do this in time to the cadence. Always, the cadence underlies and organizes the stroke.

Tempo

Tempo, unlike cadence, varies greatly. Tempo is not a function of your stroke; it is a function of the state of your body at a given time. Some nights, your body needs to work slow; sometimes fast. Some nights you will go through a variety of speeds. Always, though, these are different tempos of the same basic cadence. (Some nights you sing the song slow, other nights fast—but it's always the same song.)

Your body is an intricate, complex organism, and its actions depend on millions of processes working together. If you try to shoot faster or slower than the organism wants to work, some modules will not execute at the right time, and your shot will be poorly formed.

You can determine the speed at which to play as you walk around the table. What tempo feels easy and fluid? Count out your cadence as you walk, to see what rate of motion your body wants to adopt. Pay attention to your breathing; your body will always move easily in time to its own respiration. Your ability to discern the tempo at which you should play depends on your sensitivity to your body. Here is the element of truth in the idea of "finding" your rhythm. If, though, you have a clear knowledge of your cadence, you can "find" your speed much more easily. You can find the speed by seeing how the cadence fits with what your body is feeling.

Once you have determined the tempo that suits your body on a given occasion, keep that speed as you go into your stroke. Trying to stroke faster or slower than your body wants to move is a sure-fire way to miss—and leave yourself bewildered about why you missed. After all, you think that you lined everything up right. Maybe you did—half a second ago. *No matter how well you line up your shots, you will not shoot consistently unless you follow a solid rhythm at a pace that suits your body's needs at that moment.* That is the only way to coordinate the many mental and physical modules that must cooperate to make the shot.

Play as Dance

Understanding your rhythm starts from an analysis of your stroke, but your rhythm should underlie and coordinate all your motions. *All.* Rhythm does not start with your practice strokes and end with your follow-through. Everything you do from the moment you rise from your chair until the moment you sit back down should fit into the structure that shapes your stroke. Indeed, even your thinking and moving and breathing as you sit in your chair should keep time to the rhythm of your game.

Your stroke, after all, is just part—though the central part—of your play; you cannot wander around with no regard to the rhythm of your stroke up until the point you drop down over the table and still expect to be rhythmic in your stroke. Your stroke determines your rhythm, but your rhythm encompasses the whole of your play. Pay attention, and you will see that when players "find" their rhythms, every motion is part of the same dance. Playing in stroke, when you have "found" your rhythm, is like a ballet, everything flowing together from the time you approach the table, through each shot, from one shot to another.

We find ourselves, then, back where we started—with the pleasure of the motion. Rhythmic play, when it extends across every motion, gives us the pleasure of elegant dance. We move with grace, and our strokes are but moments of climax punctuating the dance.

Most pool players, when they are having an off night, do exactly the wrong thing: They focus on conscious controls. They become too concerned with the success of their shots, forgetting the feel of good play. Overly controlled, they fumble around the table, lumbering, wiggling, fidgeting, starting and stopping. Nothing about such play feels good—and, as we have said before, a miserable player is a miserable player.

Remember, the rhythm coordinates the motions. Put some music in your moves. Pay attention to staying rhythmic, and let the body and mind organize your motions accordingly.

PART TWO

EXPECTATIONS AND ATTITUDES

Chapter Five

Emotions: The Source of Playing at All

The Real Pro, let us call her—a famous top-five player—faced a Local Wannabe in a Women's Professional Billiards Association tournament. The Local Wannabe, whose stance seemed designed more for showing off her shapely derriere than shooting well, looked like no real challenge. Yet she was playing the Real Pro fairly even. Then she made a mistake. She called a foul on the Real Pro that nobody else, including the Real Pro, saw. They argued about it for a minute or so, then the Real Pro got angry. She didn't even bother to call the referee; she just forfeited that game to the Wannabe and ran off several games in a row to whip the Wannabe's cherished backside.

Conventional wisdom has it that emotion is dangerous to good play. This denigration of emotion probably reflects the macho posturing too common in the sport, together with ignorance of basic psychology. Whatever its source, it is quite clearly false. Motivation to act always requires emotion. Other than autonomic functions, like breathing and pumping blood, no actions happen without emotions to motivate them. Unlike robots, we only act on matters that concern us. Whenever an opportunity or event impinges on our concerns, our emotions stir us to activity. Otherwise, we remain at rest, or given to random motions with no purpose—restless. Only with emotion do we choose and pursue goals.

The question is not whether you will have emotions when you play. The question—two questions, actually: Will you be aware of your emotions, and will you modulate them to enhance the experience of playing? Perhaps many of the advisors who would have you ignore emotion do, in fact, experience little conscious emotion when they play. Lack of awareness, though, is a problem, not a model to be emulated. We know quite well, scientifically, that emotion functions whether or not we are aware of it. Having no awareness, and letting your emotions function unmodulated, hardly seems an avenue to enlightened play.

Emotions and Performance

If we think about it, we all know that pronounced emotion often helps our play. We have all, sometimes, played better because we have gotten angry at our opponents. We have all seen our game jump up a notch when several good shots in a row induce euphoria. Occasionally, a mild melancholy creates a kind of low-key calm that gives us space to play in a relaxed, almost disinterested manner. Even anxiety sometimes helps. I remember a single-elimination tournament in which I got a great win in the first round, but in the second round fell behind 5-1 in a race to nine against a guy who had trounced me in a previous tournament. My anxiety went up, and I found myself in dead stroke. I won eight of the next nine games, to end up on the happy side of a 9-6 victory.

Here's what we know scientifically about emotion and performance: Increased emotional arousal induces better concentration and more precise motor control, and therefore improves performance—up to a point. Past that point, increased emotional arousal causes excessive narrowing of focus and disruption of automatic motor control processes. The key with emotions is to have enough, but not too much.

Think of adjusting a carburetor, if you are old enough to remember carburetors. You carefully adjust the mix to approach maximum efficiency. Then you go too far, and efficiency goes down. You have to back off to regain the best performance. Even so with emotion. You have to get the right amount of emotion into your play. Eliminating emotion is about as smart as eliminating air from your engine.

A low level of emotion is only possible when you have a low level of concern. Whenever the outcome of what you are doing matters to you, you will have emotional arousal, of one sort or another, as you undertake it. The main reason we often cannot help "playing down to the level of our competition" when we face a notably inferior opponent is precisely that our emotions are not engaged. We have a hard time caring. Beating this guy won't mean much. Thus, emotional arousal is minimal, so our attention is poorly focused and our motor controls are lax. That is probably why the Wannabe was playing even with the Real Pro. The Real Pro had little emotional investment in the match. Once the Wannabe insulted the Real Pro, however, the Real Pro had a whole new motivation—to retaliate against insult. Her emotions were fully engaged, and her play improved dramatically.

The "Right Amount" of Emotion

The "right amount" of emotion depends on your particular temperament and your physical and emotional state at a given time. Different people need, or possess the capacity to handle, different amounts of arousal without going into overload. All of us vary on how much arousal we need or can handle from one occasion to another. The "cold as ice" player is not actually cold; he has a much higher threshold for handling emotion before it becomes either optimal or problematic. He needs more arousal than the rest of us to fully engage his abilities. Thus, he plays a more daring game, not from lack of emotion but from seeking more arousal than the rest of us can handle. He does not "crack under pressure" because the tension that would make most of us crazy has him humming along well within his comfortable tolerance. He is just starting to feel fully alive.

Because proper emotional engagement is highly individual, and because too little arousal is as dangerous as too much, you must be careful in adopting either "calming down" or "psyching up" exercises. You may master calming or relaxing techniques, and therefore keep yourself emotionally flaccid. You may master psyching yourself up and therefore keep your focus too narrow and your motor controls throttled. Rather than blindly applying gimmicky techniques, you need to learn to pay attention to *your own* emotional state, identify when and why *you* are unengaged or overwrought, and make modifications specific to the state in which you actually find *yourself*.

Because the right amount of emotion varies from player to player, and from one occasion to another for each player, we must guide ourselves with a general principle rather than specific instructions. The general principle is to pay attention to *your* level of emotional arousal, and try to increase it until you begin to "get tight" or fall apart. Then back off.

Modulating Your Emotions

Our emotions are barometers of the relationship between reality, as we perceive it, and our concerns. Here is how emotion happens: Some set of circumstances occurs; we appraise what those circumstances mean, positively or negatively, for our concerns; and the appraisal generates emotion, which is simply the motivation to act in a way that (experience has led us to believe) will serve our concerns. Emotion is simply the motivation to act in a specific way, under specific circumstances, to pursue something you care about.

Thus, modulating our emotions involves at least three processes: attention to the goals in relation to which the task before us matters; appraising the significance of specific circumstances for those goals; and assessing the probability that something good or bad (relative to the currently active goals) will come out of the specific situation.

The important term is "modulate." Emotions do not lend themselves to total control. We know, scientifically, that emotions begin during the processing that takes place prior to consciousness. That is, your preconscious perceptions begin a process of appraisal that sets emotion in motion before your conscious mind is aware of what's going on. Thus, we cannot start or stop emotions at will. Instead, we *become aware* of emotions after they have already started.

We cannot completely control our emotions. We can, however, modulate our emotions, indirectly and directly.

Shaping Your Emotional Climate

You can shape your emotions through two very different levels of work. The first is very general: We can deliberately cultivate the concerns we will bring to the table, and in so doing we shape the general emotional climate of our play.

The reason we can do this is simple. Few, if any, of the concerns we bring to the table have anything to do with unavoidable concerns, like survival and reproduction. Thus, our concerns in our play are concerns we can choose and cultivate. We can choose and cultivate intelligent concerns. Those concerns will determine our appraisals at the table. Specific circumstances have emotional meaning only as they impinge on our concerns; thus, the concerns we choose and cultivate will determine the emotional meanings of the events we face. If we choose wisely, we give ourselves a healthy general emotional climate.

What sorts of concerns ought we cultivate, if we want to foster optimal emotional engagement? Quite simply, concerns that make sense, given our lives, our skill levels, and the nature of the game.

Start with the last: the nature of the game. The fundamental motivation for playing is pleasure, and the underlying pleasure that makes us enjoy pool is delight in precise control of small motions—the satisfaction we take in experiencing our fine motor control causing precise, intricate, elegant shots. Oddly, humans all too often lose sight of the basic reason for doing something, letting subsidiary concerns take center stage. Pool players too often forget why the game captivated them in the first place. Keeping the pleasures of small motions central to your interests at the table will aid your emotional climate, for a simple reason: No matter what the circumstances, there is always some action available to you that can fulfill this interest. To the extent that you cultivate a central concern with the beauty of small motions, you need never be utterly distraught. Even if you have no hope of winning, no hope of avenging an insult, no hope of improving your social status among the serious players in your pool hall, you can always take delight in the motions of the game.

By the same token, some concerns make no sense, given the nature of the game. Once upon a time, when pool was strictly a male province, prowess at pool seemed somehow related to virility. That myth surely no longer makes sense. Proving your manhood is a bad motivation to bring to the table. Similarly, pool is a game of finesse, so concerns to prove your physical power have little place. Skilled players simply shake their heads at the antics of mediocre players who, having to move the cue ball a long distance around the table, wail away at it. Moving the cue ball long distances requires more finesse, not less. Proving your strength requires some sport other than pool.

Your concerns at the pool table need to be intelligent in relation to your life and skill level. A survey a few years back showed that about ninety percent of the people who take pool lessons are no longer playing within a year of their first lesson. This bespeaks stupid choices. People expect things that make no sense, then find themselves frustrated and disappointed.

What do you want pool to do for you? What makes sense, for you? How much time will you spend practicing and playing each week? How big a part of your social life will pool occupy? With whom? Why? If you give pool thirty hours a week, for example, why do you want to? Why does it matter to you? If your other interests and obligations mean that pool gets six or eight hours a week, what functions do you want it to play? It should be obvious that the thirty hour a week player has different concerns than the eight hour a week player, and what he can reasonably try to do with pool will therefore differ. Similarly, the player who has been at the game for two or three years cannot reasonably pursue the same interests as the person who has been playing ten. His reasonable hopes cannot be the same; thus, his standards of appraisal must be different.

If you choose wisely the interests and concerns you bring to the table, you insure that your appraisals instigate emotions that promote good play. That is because in most situations, you will have some concern that some action within your repertoire can serve well. If your concerns make no sense, you will often find yourself helpless and over your head.

Keeping your emotional life at the table healthy—keeping a level of emotional engagement that promotes good play—is well served by cultivating multiple interests. A great variety of other pleasures can be mixed with the basic fascination with small motions. Competition, camaraderie, mastering new skills, increasing your powers of concentration, playing your hunches, avenging insults, showing off, nurturing other players' skills or interest in the game—any number of other concerns can be profitably pursued at the table. A variety of concerns helps you emotionally, for the simple reason that you have more possible avenues to maintaining emotional engagement and satisfaction. If you cultivate multiple goals for your pool playing, something that you care about can probably be profitably pursued, no matter the conditions that prevail on a particular night. If you only have one or two goals, much of the time you will find yourself unhappy.

By cultivating a variety of clear, reasonable interests for your pool game, you give yourself a general propensity for emotional clarity, stability, and flexibility.

Controlling Your "Current Weather Conditions"

The second level at which we modulate our emotions has to do with the specific concerns we bring to the table on a given night. If our general concerns determine our emotional climate, the concerns we bring to the table on a given occasion set the conditions for that night's weather.

On different occasions, under different circumstances, different achievements give us pleasure. You need to know which of your concerns are reasonably likely to achieve fulfillment under different circumstances, and you need to be clear with yourself that the concerns available for fulfillment on a given night constitute why you are playing on this occasion. The satisfactions of rising to a challenge, humiliating an arrogant opponent, letting a good friend stay in the game without realizing we are playing down to his level, and a host of other achievements give us pleasure. All of these are emotion-rich activities. You need to pay attention to which of them you can sensibly devote yourself to under the conditions facing you.

You can also intentionally shift your emphasis, if need be. Emotional engagement is a function of the goals you actually pursue at a given time. If you find yourself lackadaisical and emotionally uninterested, look for some goal that you can get behind on this particular occasion. Winning is often the wrong goal, so far as optimal emotional engagement is concerned. When playing a notably inferior opponent, perhaps you should pay more attention to trying out new skills than to winning. When playing a notably superior opponent, perhaps pleasure in playing your best game (win or lose) should be your concern. When you find yourself getting overwrought, shift your attention to other goals than the one that has you bent out of shape.

The simple rule, then, is to find those goals that engage your attention and interest, without getting you overwrought, on a given night—or, perhaps, even at a given moment. Pay attention to your emotional states, and modulate them in pursuing pleasurable goals that engage your interests, without getting you overheated.

Cultivate multiple goals, and give precedence to those that, on the particular occasion, engage your emotions without turning the screws too tight. When one goal fails to engage you, or gets you too excited, switch your attention to a different goal.

Holding a multiplicity of goals suitable to the place of pool in your life, bringing to the table the goals that are reasonable under the circumstances, and practicing flexibility in pursuing multiple goals helps you modulate your emotions. However, the goals themselves will not generate emotion; you must couple the goals with your appraisal of how specific circumstances—and options within those circumstances—affect fulfillment of your goals. The specific emotions you will feel depend on your appraisals of specific circumstances. The most important element of modulating your specific emotions on a specific occasion is your estimation of the significance of the events you encounter.

Advice to consider only the shot before you (which is the most common advice for modulating emotions in shooting pool) ignores this fact—the shot, by itself, has little meaning. You must have an assessment of its significance for the goals that motivate you, or you will have no interest in it at all, hence no emotions, hence no performance. If you literally thought only about the shot, you would not bother to shoot it, for you would have no reason to do so. Your reason to shoot comes from your goals; and your estimation of how this shot matters in relation to those goals generates the emotion that motivates you. Thus, emotional engagement depends on both your goals and your assessment of the significance of this shot.

In one sense, you have relatively little room to manipulate your assessment of the significance of the shot: Given the goals, the significance is fairly objective. You should try to assess significance as accurately as possible, not lie to yourself about your situation. Nonetheless, we are, in fact, capable of the wildest inaccuracies in appraising our circumstances. Even within the (narrow) range of reasonable appraisals, we can be biased in helpful or unhelpful directions. *To keep your emotional engagement optimal, you need to cultivate the habit of making the most optimistic appraisal that is reasonable under the circumstances.*

As we shall see in detail in the next chapter, we can reasonably expect to play near the middle of our average ability most of the time. Sometimes we will do better, sometimes worse; but if we know our abilities, and we expect ourselves to play somewhere around the middle, we can make smart choices about our play. Our appraisals need to be based consistently on realistic expectations. "What's the situation here? What tools do I have to cope with it?" These questions need to answered honestly. However, too often we allow our most pessimistic appraisal to rule the day. "Oh, man—this is beyond me. I'm dead." Sometimes, but rarely, is this true. If you are at all competent, and if you have multiple goals in play, you can almost always find some strategy within your repertoire that will serve some purpose you care about.

You must also keep each situation in proper perspective, if your appraisal is to generate productive emotions. One common mistake of pool players is to think of significance in all-or-none terms. The shot is a winner or a loser, make or break, the key to everything. "That one shot!" we are prone to say. "If I had just made that four, I had the rack." Or, "One lucky break the guy got, and it was all over." Occasionally, but rarely, this is accurate. A pool match consists of at least a few hundred shots; only occasionally does one shot determine the outcome.

If you think in all-or-none terms, you are likely to get overly excited or lackadaisical—one way or another, you fail to appreciate the correct significance of the shot. This is one reason that players fall apart after missing one shot: They have overestimated its significance, and they get more emotional than they can handle when they miss. It is also a reason that we may make a brilliant shot, then miss the easy one that follows: We have overestimated the first shot, and having made it, we basically decide the game is over, the next shot is in the bag, and we think of the next shot as insignificant. Since we attach no significance to it, we feel nothing about it, and our concentration and motor controls go off duty.

The objective in assessing the significance of a particular shot, then, is two-fold: to be accurate (because getting a correct perspective will keep your emotions in line with reality) and to aim for the most positive outcome that you can reasonably expect (because your emotions depend in part on what you expect will happen). You may, in fact, sometimes find yourself in a hopeless situation, relative to one goal. You may find that, all things being considered, there is no good reasonably expectable positive outcome, relative to that goal. That is a time to switch goals, to keep your emotions from killing your pleasure and, therefore, your play. Under such circumstances, unless you shift goals, you will simply lose interest, collapse emotionally, and play poorly.

The specific emotions you experience in a given game result from all the factors we have discussed. However, even if we do all we can to keep our emotional weather productive, we often find ourselves in the grip of problematic emotions. What do you do then?

To understand this, you must remember that specific emotions always begin at an unconscious level. The concerns you bring to the table, the perceptions that will provide input, and the processes of appraisal are all part of the unconscious wiring you bring to the table. Humans, like all other animals, are wired to respond to circumstances faster than consciousness allows. If we did not begin to respond to circumstances instantaneously, we would have perished long ago. In the struggle to survive, action cannot wait for conscious deliberation. We evolved with exquisitely ‧ sensitive, far-reaching unconscious machinery to make appraisals and generate the emotions that motivate action.

Thus, we usually *find* ourselves *in* an emotion. Do as much as you can to develop reasonable goals, good self-knowledge, and rational appraisals of circumstances; that shapes the unconscious processes of appraisal. But those processes always begin to operate at the unconscious level. In specific circumstances, you will *become aware* of the emotions that your unconscious appraisals have generated.

There are two, and only two, elements involved in modulating emotion once it has started: body awareness and rational internal conversation.

We know scientifically that emotions involve body responses, and we know that such responses are triggered before emotions become conscious. Your unconscious appraisal has already triggered a set of bodily responses before you even become aware of your situation. That makes sense: Emotion is motivation to act, and action requires bodily motion. Thus, as soon as your unconscious appraisals generate an appraisal and emotion, your body prepares to act on it.

Relaxation techniques can help you modulate these responses. However, these suffer two shortcomings. First, they are too general, sort of like applying Ben Gay to your entire body because your right shoulder hurts. Second, they can take too much of the edge off of your motor controls and concentration. Remember that emotional engagement increases motor controls and concentration. You do not want to relax to the point of defeating your emotional engagement.

Nothing works as well as careful attention to the specific bodily responses required for good concentration. You must pay attention to the specific bodily processes required to shoot the shot before you, and relax or tighten the specific muscles groups required by the shot. Bodily awareness is crucial both to concentration and to modulating emotion. The specific bodily awareness you need compares the actual state of your body to the actual demands you face.

Though your emotions begin before you are aware of them, conscious, deliberate internal dialog can shape them. This is why you should never simply put thoughts out of your mind. If a thought occurs to you, it is a product of the mental processes that your unconscious appraisal has already set in motion. It reflects the emotional state (and therefore the motor controls and concentration processes) your unconscious appraisal has already activated. You must deal with the thought through a rational re-appraisal. You must consciously modify the unconscious appraisal from which the thought emerged. You need to enter into an internal dialog in which you consider and modify the automatic thoughts that your unconscious processes have presented to awareness.

To modulate an emotion once it has started, you must put these two things—rational internal dialog and good body awareness—together. You must use a rational internal dialog to determine what, realistically, you need to do; and you must then use your awareness of the bodily sensations needed to accomplish it to interrogate and change your current bodily state. Thus, you recognize the bodily processes that your unconscious processes have set in motion; you decide whether the actions to which those processes are moving you are appropriate; and you modify your bodily processes to accord with what your rational appraisal has determined that you really need to do.

Once a specific emotion starts, you cannot simply negate it. Pretending it does not exist simply allows it to operate unconsciously. You can do a great deal to determine what kinds of emotions you will undergo by deliberately cultivating intelligent concerns, by thinking clearly about which goals you are pursuing on a given occasion, and by cultivating flexibility in switching between multiple concerns. You can cultivate habits of sound appraisal. All of that shapes the wiring that will generate emotions. Nonetheless, the specific emotions you experience are not entirely within conscious control at the moment they occur, since they always begin at the unconscious level. You must cultivate good awareness of what emotions have been generated, and you need to cultivate habits of modulating those emotions through good body awareness and a sound internal dialog. The dumbest thing you can do is to ignore feelings that have been generated. The reason this is dumb? Those feelings are shaping the state of your motor controls and mental attentiveness. Ignore them, and your conscious and unconscious efforts are simply at cross purposes.

The Moral of the Story

The lesson of this chapter is to cultivate optimal emotional engagement. An emotionless player is no player at all. How well you tune your emotional engagement will depend upon your self-awareness and psychological skill.

Players differ not only in their physical skills; they differ in their self-awareness and capacity for self-modulation. You can cultivate awareness of multiple goals and awareness of your state of emotionality. You can cultivate flexibility in shifting the weight you give to each goal on a specific occasion. You can develop your capacity for perspective on the significance of each situation. Since emotional engagement is fundamental to concentration and motor controls, developing such self-knowledge and skill at self-modulation is as important as working on your draw shot.

For all of our efforts in this chapter, we have only touched on one crucial element of the appraisals that will generate emotions. Your goals and your assessment of the situation do not fully determine your emotions. Equally important is your prediction of possible outcomes. That is a matter of confidence, which deserves a chapter of its own—to which we now turn.

Chapter Six

Confidence: The Security of Accurate Expectations

A confident player, we all know, enjoys a higher probability of success than a frightened one. Certainly we feel better when we play with confidence. We play with greater ease, fluidity, and rhythm. Accordingly, confidence, like concentration, constitutes a staple of advisories on the mental game. Like concentration, the notion is poorly explained and poorly understood.

Listen to this advice from one of the Bibles of the sport: "Try to play with confidence, even if you have little reason for having any. The sooner you act like a good player, the sooner you'll become one."

Unfortunately, this advice is as misguided as it is common.

Confidence is a subjective feeling, the emotion we feel when we anticipate success. The word literally means "with faith." Confidence is an anticipatory feeling: a feeling that results from a prediction we make. However, this prediction may be more or less reasonable; confidence can be induced by realistic expectations or by illusion.

Confidence induced by reality tends to be stable; confidence induced by illusion tends to be unstable. When confidence falters, we become anxious, tentative, and frustrated. Confidence based on illusion, then, sets us up for all sorts of feelings that destroy good play.

Lack of confidence certainly undermines both the pleasure and the quality of our play. If we do not anticipate success, we do not

71

feel particularly good. Inflating your sense of self falsely solves the problem only temporarily, however, and badly. Confidence based on illusion is bound to fail and bring disruptive feelings in its wake. To solve the problem, we need to understand how to avoid illusion and arrive at reality-based confidence.

Confidence and Self-Image

The popular notion of "self esteem" has infected advice on confidence in sports. A fair number of people—from self-help authors to inspirational speakers to scientifically incompetent therapists to sports "psychologists"—make a fair amount of money selling psychological snake oil. Boost your self-esteem, get rid of your negative self-image, learn to affirm yourself—such advice abounds.

The idea is that confidence derives from one's general sense of self, and a negative self-image undermines confidence. Intuitively, this seems plausible. The idea owes its popularity almost entirely to its plausibility, not to any evidence that it is true. The research base was never strong, and in recent years research has largely discredited the whole idea.

Simply put, performance does not correlate with self-image. Twenty years of (very robust) research shows that almost everyone has an unrealistically positive self-image. Almost everyone's self-image exceeds his or her performance. Furthermore, in the last few years, research aimed directly at testing hypotheses about self-esteem has shown that some highly successful people have terrible self-esteem, while some of the biggest failures enjoy very high self-regard.

With pool players, you can see the discrepancy between self-esteem and performance quite easily, in the phenomenon of excuses. Excuses are simply the way you explain the discrepancy between your imagined abilities—your self-image—and your actual play. You have a positive (but false) image of yourself as a player; but you fail to live up to it, so you make excuses.

In one sense, most pool players have too much confidence: Our images of our abilities are falsely inflated. The margin of inflation is revealed by the frequency and magnitude of excuses. Since excuses are the way we explain the fact that our actual play falls short of our self-images, the frequency and magnitude of excuses indicates the gap between image and reality. One reason we find ourselves in trouble at the table is that reality deflates our false confidence. Improving your confidence in yourself as a player will not necessarily solve that problem, if your confidence is not based in reality.

If positive self-image offers no panacea, getting rid of "negative self talk"—another staple of advisors on the mental game—is no simple cure for lack of confidence, either. A basic technique of behavior modification, "flooding," relies on filling your mind with images of your most feared outcome. A related technique, from the psychodynamic perspective, requires that you imagine your worst case scenario, and then work on accepting the consequences that would follow if it happened to be true. Once you do this, your anxiety decreases, and you are free to think of better possible outcomes. A widely used, successful technique for helping musicians deal with performance anxiety is to have them "overload" their conscious thoughts with negative self-images! As if all this were not enough to prove that negativity can, in fact, promote confidence, we might note that most religions have long taught the value of humility.

Research has established that, left to our natural inclinations, all of us believe we are good at what we care about and that we control our destinies. We will discount information to the contrary, until we find ourselves failing in ways that we can no longer ignore. That is why our self-images tend to be overly positive.

Most of us do not suffer a lack of confidence; we suffer from unstable, ill-founded confidence. The tentativeness, fear, and frustration that most advisors claim confidence should conquer is, in fact, most often the result of unstable confidence. It is the result of facing situations in which we have reason to believe we cannot perform as we imagine we ought. As we anticipate a discrepancy between our positive images of our ability and what we really have reason to think we may do, we recognize the high probability of embarrassment, of being forced to accept painful truths that falsify our good feelings about our abilities. When we go ahead and "confidently" undertake something beyond our ability and fail, our confidence plummets. We try to save our good feelings by making excuses. We nonetheless find ourselves facing the fact that our beliefs about our abilities do not correctly predict our performance. This does not promote further confidence.

The only aspect of self-image that seems to have much effect on performance is our beliefs about how we will be perceived by others—*not* how we think of ourselves, but how we think others will see us. This issue, though, is dependent on the specific conditions under which we find ourselves undergoing scrutiny—who is evaluating us and why. We will discuss this issue when we turn our attentions to competition, in the next chapter.

Effective Confidence

If confidence that helps your performance is not a matter of self-image, what is it? Effective confidence is situation specific: It is an assessment of the specific resources at your disposal to meet a concrete, clearly-defined challenge facing you at a given time. *Effective confidence is a matter of knowing what needs to be done, knowing what tools to use, and knowing that those tools are adequate to the task.* Your beliefs about your "self" are simply too general to do you much good at this level. You can believe you are a great person, or a talented player, without knowing which shot needs to be made or that it falls within your skills.

Confidence always derives from a prediction you make about the probability of success. Predictions based upon sound knowledge of what a situation requires, and what tools you have at your disposal to meet the challenge, generate rational confidence. Because this confidence is based upon a reasonable prediction, it is stable. Reality will reinforce such confidence, not negate it.

The stability of your confidence is a function of the soundness of your beliefs about what you are likely to be able to do. Achieving stable, effective confidence depends on two things: accurate self-knowledge and reasonable expectations.

We begin with the latter. "Success" is a relative term; it always requires some goal, some standard of achievement, to give it meaning. What will count as success? What you expect yourself to achieve is crucial to predicting success. If you expect yourself to play like a pro, when in fact you are a B player, you will never development rational, stable confidence. You will always expect of yourself what you cannot do.

Most of us do not fall prey to that particular error—thinking we are pros when we are not. However, we do make the mistake of pegging our expectations to our best possible performance. Conventional wisdom encourages us to do this—to aim at "peak performance." Many advisors tell you that if you can do something once, you ought to be able to do it all the time. They advise you to envision your best performance and make that the standard of your self-expectations. Indeed, some pool advisors seem to think that "confidence" simply *is* believing you will achieve peak performance. This makes no sense, psychological or otherwise.

Contrary to that conventional wisdom, it is reasonable to expect yourself to play at about the middle of your ability most of the time. It is not reasonable to expect yourself to achieve "peak performance" consistently. As a simple matter of logic, your best performance is the one that is better than all your other performances. Thus, it is logically impossible that every shot will be your best.

As a practical matter, variance is a fact of nature. Simple, non-living items, like steel rods, vary in size, flexibility, and structural integrity (hence in performance) under different physical conditions. Engineers know this. In designing machines and structures they have to calculate "tolerances" based on assumptions of the weak, not peak, performance of their materials. Otherwise, their creations would fail under real-world conditions. Pegging your definitions of success to your peak performance is about as wise as buying a car or living in a building designed with no tolerances.

With complex living organisms, the situation is much worse than with steel rods. Complex living organisms vary in literally millions of ways from one circumstance to the next, with radical ramifications for what is possible at any given time. Because you are alive, because you are not a robot, you simply cannot perform the same way all the time. Human bodies—and human minds—display extremely wide tolerances, because they must be capable of performing the many, varied uses to which we put them. Thus, we simply cannot avoid wide variance in performance.

Your predictions about how you will perform must be based on your average expectable performance, not on your best possible performance. You increase the stability of your confidence if your choices of how to shoot, and your expectations of what you will achieve, derive from your average expectable ability—not from your absolute best.

Roughly two-thirds of your shots will fall somewhere between 35 and 65 percent of your best ability. About fifteen, maybe twenty, percent of your shots will fall between 65 and 97 percent of your ability. Realistically, you will achieve "peak performance" on about 2 percent of your shots.

Thus, if your expectations rely on your estimation of your peak performance, about 98% of the time you will fail. If you are not to undermine your confidence, you simply must base your predictions of your performance on your expectable performance, not your peak performance.

The easiest way to "lose confidence" is to expect of yourself something that is highly unlikely, then make some excuse why it did not work. You start thinking, "I could have done that, but didn't—my game is off tonight." You lose concentration, and you begin analyzing the challenges you face half-heartedly, convinced—erroneously—that you are "off" your game. You are not off your game; rather, you have unrealistic expectations which (because they are unrealistic) you fail to fulfill. You destroy your own confidence.

To illustrate, suppose you come to the table in a game of nine ball, with five balls left on the table, laid out in an open pattern. If, in fact, you generally run out from the five (assuming no clusters) about twenty percent of the time, you should realize that you have about a twenty percent chance of running out. Suppose that you can generally make a three ball run about eighty percent of the time. If you expect yourself to run out, chances are very good that you will disappoint yourself. Suppose you make four balls and miss the nine. In fact, you have performed quite well, relative to your abilities. You should be pleased with yourself; you are on your game. Sure, your opponent may step up and tap the nine ball in, but this is no reason for you to lose confidence. Quite the contrary. You know that, in fact, your skills are showing themselves quite well. You may or may not win the match; but if you do not, it will be because the other guy played better, not because you are off your game. Losing to better players should not shake your confidence; better players ought to beat you.

Of course, you can never have reasonable expectations unless you have an honest sense of your exact skills. You simply must know your own abilities; you must know what is within your normal range. You have every right to be confident when a situation calls for a shot that, within your average expectable play, you are most likely to make. Indeed, rational confidence is the feeling you get in precisely this situation.

Scientists know that everyone suffers what they call "observer bias." We all tend to see what we want to see. To counter observer bias, scientists keep careful logs of everything that is done and measured every day. When an experiment is finished and reported in the scientific journals, other scientists must be able to replicate the results before they are accepted as true. Pool players generally do not make any deliberate efforts to keep objective records of our own abilities. Thus, our "observer bias" tends to make us overestimate our abilities. We make a tough shot half a dozen times, and we decide we can "make it in our sleep"—forgetting that we missed the same shot ten times the same night. We then miss that shot to lose a match later in the week, and we "can't believe it." We curse ourselves, or make up some excuse, and claim we played badly. In fact, we really miss that shot more than we make it. Our moaning is the result of false beliefs about our ability, derived from observer bias.

The best way to get an accurate sense of your abilities is to act like a good scientist: keep good records. A "pool journal" is an excellent idea.

The Pool Journal

An accurate, honest pool journal can tell you your current skill level exactly.

A pool journal is a private diary of your practice and play. Every time you practice or play, you need to take objective notes on what happens.

For the journal to be meaningful, you need to establish certain drills or exercises that you will do regularly over a period of time. Any good drill will do; the point is to do it regularly enough to generate an informative measurement.

For instance, if you are working on position play off your draw shot, you choose a drill that tests this accurately—say, lining up seven balls across the middle of the table and trying to sink them in the top corner pockets, while keeping the cue ball below the middle of the table. You take ball in hand and start to shoot; as soon as you miss, or let the cue ball go above mid-table, you start over. The numbers of balls you sink in each run gets recorded. If you do this drill ten times a day, three days a week, for a month, you have over 120 runs recorded.

Once you have these numbers, it is a simple matter to sit down with a piece of graph paper and chart your performance. Your graph should have seven blocks across the horizontal (that is, the bottom)—for runs of one ball, two balls, three balls, etc. Above each block along the horizontal, color in one block for each run you made that matches that number. Thus, if you make 8 one ball runs, 12 two ball runs, 26 three ball runs, etc., you end up with 8 blocks colored above the first horizontal block, 12 above the second, 26 above the third, and so on. The result is a precise chart of your ability.

You can go further and figure out your exact percentages: What percent of the time did you make four ball runs, five ball runs, etc.? To do this, simply divide the number of blocks above a given horizontal block by the total number of runs. That is, if you have made, say, twenty-six three-ball runs, and you have recorded 120 runs, you divide 26 by 120—and find that you make three ball runs, on this drill, about twenty-two percent of the time.

You can figure your average run by adding up all the balls you've sunk, then dividing by the total number of runs. Thus, if you have made, say, 612 balls in 120 runs, you have averaged 5.1 balls per run.

Perhaps you want to work on a specific shot. You shoot that shot twenty-five times a day, four days a week, for a month, and you have over 400 shots. Divide the number of times you made the shot by the total number of times you tried it, and you know precisely what "percentage shot" that is for you.

You should probably also include in your practice a certain number of racks of your current favorite game—say, ten racks of nine-ball every day. Break, shoot until you miss, and record the number of shots you have made in that rack. By the end of the month, you will be able to see exactly what you can expect of yourself from the break.

If you keep your journal when you play matches, record the number of balls in each run, how you sat down each turn, what safeties you made or missed, what clusters you successfully broke up, and the like.

If you practice systematically, and keep your journal honestly, you end up with a very clear sense of exactly what you can expect from yourself. The more extensive your practice—the more shots you keep tabs on—the more comprehensive your self-knowledge. If you study your journal carefully, you also know what works best for you. For instance, you may find that (at a given time) you are averaging half a ball better when playing follow shots than draw shots. Knowing this, you can choose follow shots over draw shots, when the choice presents itself, and thus increase your confidence.

Keeping a good journal is simply a matter of *knowing your toolkit*. Confidence is a matter of knowing what tools you possess, knowing when to use them, and knowing that you can rely on them. If you keep a good journal, and your practice is extensive, you have a sound knowledge of your repertoire. Thus, when you approach the table, you can choose your shots and strategies on the basis of the tools you really possess. You can make a rational prediction of what to expect of yourself. You can be confident, because your choices are based on clear knowledge.

Confidence, Probability, and Your Current Skills

Confidence turns on your faith in your ability, and stable faith originates in good information. It requires reasonable expectations and well-grounded self-knowledge. From this, it follows that confidence, rightly understood, is relative. Confidence is relative to your goals and abilities.

People talk as if confidence were an all-or-none affair—you believe you will make a shot or not, complete a run or not, win a match or not. In fact, confidence comes in all shades, about all sorts of things. A sophisticated level of confidence factors in multiple goals and rests on calculations of probabilities, not absolutes.

Since the bodies of living creatures exhibit wide tolerances, and thus a wide variance characterizes our performances, your predictions of your performance need to be made in terms of probabilities. Your confidence derives from a probabilistic expectation, reasonable to your level of play. So, for instance, when you approach the nine-ball table that has five well-spaced balls left, you need to base your decisions on realistic percentages. "Let's see: Generally, I run out from the five about twenty percent of the time. But in this case, the five shots involved would be about an 80 percent shot, two sixty percent shots, a forty, and a ninety, given my skills. Kinda tough." If you want to get mathematical, you could even calculate that, for you, the probability of completing this particular five ball run is about ten percent (.80 x .60 x .60 x .40 x .90=.10368). However, perhaps you recognize that you could shoot the first two shots, then you would have the possibility of a safety that is a ninety percent shot for you. The probability of completing this sequence is over forty percent—not great, but better. If you succeeded at this, you would come back to the table with only three balls to shoot. Perhaps, though, the first shot allows for a safety that is an eighty percent shot for you. If your goal in this instance is to win, your choice is clear: shoot the first shot as a safety. If, though, your goal is to try out new skills or to challenge yourself, you might choose either of the other options.

In either case, your prediction of your performance has to be formed relative to your goal—to win or to try a new skill or to challenge yourself—and the percentages. Thus, how you feel about the effort—your confidence or lack thereof—will be relative to these decisions.

You keep your confidence high by making good decisions and evaluating the results reasonably. You choose a goal that suits your motivation for this particular event, and you use your knowledge of your skill level to set your strategy. If, in fact, you have about a forty percent chance of completing your planned strategy, and you only get about halfway to the goal before missing, you recognize that you played perfectly well, relative to your skills. Knowing this, your failure does not cause your confidence to plummet.

The importance of multiple motivations once again becomes clear. To keep confidence high, you need to set a goal with a high likelihood of success. But goals depend on motivation. If you have cultivated a variety of motivations—not just the motivation to win—you can usually find a goal that is meaningful to you that is within your abilities. Sometimes the goal may be as simple as stroking smoothly on a shot that you sometimes try to force. If you set goals that mean something to you, that you have a high probability of achieving, you keep your confidence high. If you cannot entertain multiple motivations, but always have to win, you will often set goals that you cannot reasonably expect to meet. Your confidence, quite rightly, will falter. You will not enjoy your play. In the worst case, you will fold, just because you do not fulfill some fantasy you have about how great you ought to be.

The Banality of Confidence

Confidence, quite simply, is knowing what you can realistically expect of yourself in a given situation, expecting it, and setting your goals accordingly. Achieving and maintaining confidence requires no tricks or gimmicks, no psychobabble or hocus-pocus, no mystical transportation into spiritual nether-worlds.

"I have a problem with confidence. I really let my low self-esteem undermine my play, and I don't live up to my potential." That's a common excuse, and an excuse is all that it is. When someone says this, usually, he is really saying, "I have illusions about how good I am. When I actually play, I don't live up to them. I get frustrated, despondent, and self-punitive. As a result, I lose concentration, and my game goes to pieces." Most of the time, these illusions originate in expecting yourself always to play every shot the way you played it the best shot you ever made in your life. That is irrational, and deadly, besides.

If you are honest about your ability, your expectations and your performance will match up most of the time. Thus, you will feel satisfied with the majority of your shots, and you will relax and feel good. Your rhythm will flow naturally and your confidence will grow. Your mental state will promote, not undermine, your play. You will generally lose only to those players who by rights ought to beat you (those whose skills are better than yours). In fact, you will beat a lot of people whose skills exceed yours, because their mental attitude (aimed at peak performance) will be weaker than yours.

Some nights you will play as if you ought to be a pro. Those nights are bliss. Everything is just right, and the game of your wildest Walter Mitty dreams is the game you play. Wonderful. Enjoy it. But don't take it as the new standard of your self-adulation, thinking this is how you ought to play all the time.

Some nights will be horrible. You will have other things eating at you, you will be tired and tense, your eyes won't work quite right, your judgment will be off, whatever. No big deal. You are a living organism, and you cannot avoid such nights. Don't take it as the new standard of your self-reproach, deciding you are a horrible player who ought to sell his cue and take up shuffleboard.

Be honest about your general level of ability, plan your shots and strategies accordingly, and be delighted when most of your shots fulfill your ordinary performance. Set your goals to serve motivations that make sense for your level of ability, under just the circumstances you face. Shape your predictions of your performance to accord with what your skills entitle you to achieve. If you do these simple, straightforward things, your predictions about your play will be sound, success at your goals will be within your grasp, and you will be confident of doing what you predict. Even better, your confidence will usually prove well-founded, and your success make it all the more solid and stable.

Chapter Seven

Competition: Playing to Win

If you want to get from pool the most it has to offer you, you need to be able to play for many reasons, under many circumstances. Anyone serious about the game, though, wants to include competition in his reasons to play. When you compete, your overriding goal is to win.

The key term here is "overriding." In competition, winning should not become your only goal, even though it becomes the main one. You sustain your interest in many other goals, but *in service to* winning. Forget all other goals, and your chances of winning decline.

What do I mean by that? Consider an analogy.

Suppose your wedding anniversary is approaching. You and your spouse have been taking each other for granted, and the reason you got married in the first place has fallen off your radar screen. The day-to-day stuff goes all right, but the spark has disappeared. You might as well be roommates or business partners, for all the romance you feel. You decide that on this anniversary, you want to rekindle the feelings that made you fall in love in the first place. That is your overriding goal.

To do that, you want to show your spouse how much you appreciate her (or him, as the case may be). You want her to feel loved and valued. Thus, you think through the things she likes and plan a wonderful evening, including reservations at her favorite expensive restaurant. You go to the jewelry store to choose a special gift. Because your overriding goal is to rekindle the feelings that led her to fall in love with you in the first place, you undertake each of these tasks in certain ways.

For instance, the goal of buying a gift: Because of your overriding goal, you go to the jewelry store and buy something a bit extravagant that she will enjoy—a beautiful necklace, say—rather than going to Sears and buying something judicious that she needs. Or the goal of having dinner: You go to her favorite excellent restaurant, not to some run-of-the-mill place or to some place you want to try yourself because you have heard it is good. When your food arrives, hers is perfect but yours is okay but not quite right. No matter; you do not complain or send it back—you keep the news to yourself and enjoy her pleasure. Your goal is not the quality of your food, but the quality of her experience. Or consider the goal of having a lively dinner conversation: You choose conversation topics to let her know how special she is. If your goal were just ordinary communication, you might talk about work or the kids or some dissatisfaction you have been feeling in the marriage. Because your overriding goal is to rekindle the spark between you, you tell her what you love and appreciate about her, things that you tend to take for granted on a daily basis. You reminisce about your best times, and you talk about fun, romantic things you can do in the future. You recapture her romantic imagination.

In each case, your subsidiary goals—a gift, dinner, conversation— take their shape because of your overriding goal. Even so with competition in pool. Your subsidiary goals—pleasure in the strokes themselves, organizing your thinking and working to a good rhythm, meeting a challenge, maybe even trying out new skills if the occasion arises, and so forth—do not vanish. Rather, they take specific shapes because winning is your overriding goal. You do them differently than you would if you were not out to win.

Winning is a worthy goal. It should not be your main goal all the time, but when it is, you need to be clear about that. "Winning" is a matter of pursuing your subsidiary goals in a particular way. You cannot win simply by intending to win, any more than you can rekindle the spark in your marriage simply by announcing that you want to do so. You have to be clear about your subsidiary activities and pursue them in service to your overriding goal. In pool, you must keep sight of the elements of play—why you play at all—and pursue them in a particular form. Lose sight of the pleasures of small motions, and you might as well try to reinvigorate your marriage by walking up to your wife and saying, "Feel like you used to feel, now!"

What Makes Competition Different?

Why do we compete? What is the concern behind winning? What are we trying to accomplish by winning, that makes competition different from other kinds of play?

Competition differs from ordinary play in two ways, and they reinforce each other. Obviously, the stakes are different; but more importantly, in competition you are involved in a social process that involves your being evaluated. Social evaluation—being judged by others—takes very different forms in competition than other times. Whether or not you are playing for money, one thing that is at stake in competition is how you will be evaluated. Competition determines your relative status in the world of players in your locale. For most of us—those who do not depend on pool for our income, and who have sense enough not to bet money we cannot afford to lose—money is just an objective measure of status. Winning or losing money just gives a concrete form to bragging rights.

Whether you are competing informally or playing in a league match or a tournament, who wins (and how) has an impact on your standing in a specific part of your social world: the world of people in your life who know and care about pool. When you compete, you always have an audience, directly and indirectly. Directly, you have at least one person evaluating your every move: the person you are playing against. Indirectly, you have everyone he (or she) will tell about the match and everyone who will ask you about it. In league play, you have everyone in the league who is keeping up with the standings. Likewise in tournaments.

"Winning," then, is a matter of establishing status. Who's who around here? The concern behind the desire to win is concern with how you are regarded. We want to win to establish ourselves at higher levels of esteem within the community of players than we would enjoy if we lost.

That makes competition matter. It both raises our level of play and causes us problems. Social evaluation is one of the well-documented, extensively studied elements of sport psychology. Knowing that you are being evaluated, that your standing as a player rides on the outcome, improves play—unless you believe that you are unlikely to live up to the standards of evaluation. If you believe that you are unlikely to live up to the standards of evaluation, you will play poorly.

The effect of competition on our play, then, is always relative—relative to the standards by which we expect to be judged, and to our estimation of our likelihood of measuring up. Research into the "home field advantage" shows this clearly. At home, we are more likely to get the benefit of the doubt; we know that our fans will tend to skew their judgments in our favor. Thus, we are more likely to be evaluated well. However, for championship teams playing at home in an effort to repeat as champions, the home field advantage vanishes. Why? Because the fans' expectations are higher, so players know there is a greater risk of failing to meet them.

Most advice on how to compete aims to do one (or both) of two things: Increase your belief that you will measure up, or decrease your belief that you will fail. These sound like two sides of the same thing, but they are not—quite. Psychologically, people differ in which matters to them more. Some people need to establish themselves as socially dominant; for them, winning is the most important thing. Other people are more egalitarian. They do not care much about being dominant, but they do not wish to be dominated. For them, the important thing is not to lose.

Advice that aims to boost your confidence aims at the first goal—believing you can measure up. Advice to keep negative or "defeatist" thoughts out of your mind aim at the second. Believe you will win (and thus raise or maintain your status); don't believe you will lose (and thus fall in status). Those constitute the two elements of good competitive psychology.

"Competitive pressure," then, is the pressure of establishing status. The psychology of competition is not about the game itself; it is the psychology of your concerns about status. (That, by the way, is why pro players getting their first shot at playing on television, or amateur players making it to their first finals in a tournament where an audience is present, tend to feel extra pressures: They are being evaluated by a wider audience than usual.) *Any pool advice about competing that fails to address status concerns fails to teach you what matters about competition.*

A good competitive mind set allows you to do your best, under the pressure of status concerns. Everyone knows that, to compete well, you have to be able to maintain an optimal belief in succeeding, and avoid self-defeating beliefs that you are doomed. However, understanding how to achieve that psychology can be better or worse. Some of the advice is very bad. As we have seen, irrational confidence sets you up for disaster. Keeping negative thoughts out of your mind (rather than recognizing and addressing them) puts your conscious and unconscious processes at odds with each other. Pretending that you are not competing, trying to ignore the fact that social evaluation is the underlying issue of competition, is simply stupid. It guarantees that you will never understand how to compete.

The questions we have to answer, then, are these: What psychologically sound processes keep confidence sound? What psychologically sound processes prevent defeatism? What challenges to those processes do status concerns bring about?

The Fundamental Challenge of Competition

Competition offers many challenges, but underlying them all is the quest for status. The corollary *problem* is consciousness of status and concern about the impact of your play on your status.

With concerns about status working on our heads, we are prone to self-consciousness. Competition is not just about the game; it is about *you* and how you will be regarded. Watching yourself—asking yourself, "So how do I look, what are people thinking"—comes easily. Such questions arise when we suffer a conflict between how we *want* to be seen and how we think we *will be* seen. Fearing that we are not presenting ourselves well, we become overly vigilant, watching ourselves and "trying." That is, we attempt to exert conscious, deliberate control over our every move.

As we have seen, excessive conscious controls destroy our play. They disrupt the smooth workings of our motor controls, they disrupt rhythm, they undermine the automatic functioning of all the skills we have carefully built, they narrow our mental processes so that we are not free to think about our most sophisticated strategies and possibilities—in short, they put us at odds with ourselves, disrupting everything that makes us play our best. When we become self-conscious, conscious controls reach a destructive zenith.

Unfortunately, "Don't be self-conscious" is sort of like, "Don't think about an elephant." You probably will not avoid self-consciousness by telling yourself not to be self-conscious. Rather, you avoid self-consciousness by addressing the conflict between how you want to be seen and how you believe you will be seen. You only become self-conscious if you have reason to doubt that you can measure up; this arises when your wish to be seen a certain way conflicts with what you believe you can expect. Obviously, there are two sides to this problem: Your wish—that is, your image of how you will be ideally be seen—and your fear.

Effective confidence takes care of reasonable fear; it will take care of the conflict between your wish and your fear only if your wishes are realistic. We have already studied the fundamentals of effective confidence; we will turn to a direct application of confidence to the competitive situation shortly. For now, we need to study the issue of how we wish to be seen—and how it can undermine play.

The most effective way to destroy your competitive ability, the most widespread source of crippling anxiety, is unrealistic wishes. That is, you have a certain image of how you ought to be regarded, which bears little resemblance to your true level of ability. You convince yourself that you ought to be able to play up to this fantasy. When you practice or goof around, you can exaggerate your good moments and dismiss your bad ones in your mind—the phenomenon of "observer bias" we discussed in the last chapter. You edit your sense of reality to suit your self-image. However, when you compete, your status will be determined by the play that others see; they are not likely to edit your play in the way you usually do. You will, in fact, play as you really play, not as you imagine. Your status will, in fact, be affected. To the precise degree that your self-image is unreasonable, you will face a serious conflict between what you wish and what you have reason to expect.

When your imagined status significantly exceeds your ability, you will not be able to sustain effective confidence: You have no good reason to expect yourself to live up to what you wish. As soon as your play starts negating your fantasy status, you get anxious. Aiming to forestall (reasonably) expected defeat, you start "trying harder." You become self-conscious. Thus, you play less well than you ordinarily do. You compete poorly. You do not show your true skills.

When this happens, you blame your failure on a "lack of confidence" or inability to handle competitive anxiety. After all, your experience tells you—partly accurately, partly as a result of observer bias—that you play better when you practice or goof around than when you compete. The problem, though, is not competition. The problem is that your self-image is wrong, and competition, unlike practice or goofing around, does not permit your creative editing. You are correct in saying that you compete poorly. In fact, competition makes you self-conscious—but not because that is the nature of competition. You become self-conscious because competition shows clearly the discrepancy between your wishes and how you really play. Paradoxically, you play worse in competition than a person of your skills really ought to. You play worse than you normally do, because you believe you are better than you are.

This problem resembles a widespread psychological problem known as Narcissistic Personality Disorder (NPD). For a person with NPD, the most important task is propping up an inflated self-image. The problem is that the self-image bears only passing resemblance to reality. Lacking a firm basis in reality, the self-image is unstable. It tends to collapse with some frequency, plunging the narcissist into depression, defensive anger, and despair.

When we have unrealistic notions about our pool playing, we suffer something I call NPPD—narcissistic pool player disorder. If you suffer from NPPD, you have an inflated image of your ability, and you spend a lot of energy (and talk) convincing yourself and everyone else that it is true. You also spend a good bit of time depressed, irritated, and dejected about your game.

When you compete, you fear (correctly) that the match will put the lie to your self-image. You find this terrifying. A person with NPD believes deep in his heart that his true self is not good enough, so he has to pretend to be more than that. The person with NPPD, likewise. The NPPD player cannot look truthfully at his skills and form expectations that make sense, because he believes he is not good enough. As soon as he steps to the table, the first shot that goes against him deflates his exaggerated self-image and casts him into his unconscious belief that he is terrible. Thus, the conflict between wish and fear is at its apex. He tries to pump himself up, with all sorts of self-affirmations. But the fact is, he simply cannot play up to the status he imagines he deserves. No matter how he tries, he faces this conflict. He becomes self-conscious, tries hard, and defeats his real ability.

This scenario, or some milder version of it, lies behind most psychological problems of competition. Contrary to the usual psychological snake oil, competitive problems rarely come from low self-esteem. Quite the contrary. Most people who compete poorly suffer unrealistic images of how well they play. They think their status should be higher than they really deserve. Competition will prove that they do not deserve what they wish for. Caught in the conflict between wish and fear, they become self-conscious and undermine their own skills.

The Basic Solution

The basic solution has two sides. First, get your expectations in line with reality. Form a reasonable sense of what you can expect of yourself, relative to the competition. Go into the match expecting something you have good reason to believe is within your power. Second, remember that competition *establishes* status. Go into competition to *find out* where you deserve to rank—not to prove that the status in your head is correct. The purpose of competition is *not* to shore up your self-image. The purpose of competition is to find out something about yourself. That is why we say that competition *tests* us

Getting an accurate sense of what to expect of yourself requires the kind of self-knowledge we discussed in the last chapter. You need to know, honestly, what your skills are. Notice that effective confidence and a reasonable set of expectations flow from the same source: accurate knowledge. If your sense of your deserved status is in line with your skills, and you have arrived at that sense of deserved status by careful study of your game, your expectations for yourself and your confidence in yourself go hand in hand. The conflict between your wish and your fear is, on most occasions, minimal.

If you have an accurate sense of how you ought to be regarded, and you have the effective confidence that goes with it, you will most often perform accordingly. If you know how your skills stack up against the competition, you know the kind of status you ought to have. If you are able to accept that, you can make full use of your skills. You will not suffer a conflict between what you believe your status should be and what you expect yourself to accomplish.

People who cannot look at their play honestly generally fear that they are not good enough. Good enough for what? If you expect pool to make up for your problems in life, to compensate for what you believe are your failings in your social world, you probably will never be good enough for that. Very few people gain enough status from pool to be forgiven their other social shortcomings. If you expect to enjoy the adulation of everyone who watches you play, you have a slim chance of that—unless you happen to be a top pro. You will never be good enough to be better than you are. Whatever your level of skill, though, you are good enough to enjoy the game. Honest acceptance of your skill level, and the status it will earn you, poses no threat to that.

You simply must remember that competition establishes status; that is, it shows who is better than whom. Thus, you should not expect yourself to win every match. All of the players in the room, except one, are wrong when they think they are the best. If you go into competition to find out your status, rather than to confirm the status in your head, you are freed from internal conflict. When your sense of your abilities accords with your aims for status, you will be free to play *your* best possible pool in most of your matches, to find out exactly what status that skill level will give you. Free of preconceived notions of exalted status, you will win the vast majority of those matches you ought to win. You will even win some matches against players who, by rights, ought to beat you. You will beat some better opponents precisely because you will be mentally competent to excel against their weaknesses, to exploit the times when their games are off.

No one should ever be ashamed of losing to a better player. Losing to a better player is not a failure. It is information about where you stack up—which is supposed to be the point of competition in the first place. If you cannot accept yourself for the player that you are, you will constantly undermine your own play. If you accept yourself for the player that you are, you can keep your skills and your expectations in line. That is the best recipe for competing well—and for knowing, truthfully, without self-serving excuses, where you need to improve.

The basic solution to the fundamental challenge of competition, then, is to go into every match with a realistic sense of your skills. Expect the match to establish accurately who is the better player, at least on this night. Evaluate your play in terms of whether you are showing your skills fairly. Accept that the match will tell you, as well as everyone else, something about your status. Do not get invested in some fantasy in your head about what you think you deserve. If you have some preconceived fantasy, you may in fact be playing very well, but losing, and you may therefore become self-conscious and fall apart. You need to learn that your job is to continue playing well, not to fulfill some preconceived image.

Remembering Pleasure

Winning is the goal of competition. But a miserable player is a miserable payer, and if you have lost touch with the pleasures of play, you play less well than your skills merit. Indeed, if you have lost touch with the pleasures of your bodily motions, that is a pretty good sign you have gotten out of your body, into your head—that you are trying to play the fantasy game you imagine you should, rather than the game you really can.

When you play your best, you concentrate well, and you move to a steady rhythm. Remember that concentration is always about the body. Remember that rhythm is the medium of bodily coordination. Concentration choreographs your motions, and rhythm executes the choreography. Neither concentration nor rhythm can happen without rich body awareness. Rich body awareness, in the presence of good concentration and well-formed rhythm, simply *is* pleasant. If you are not enjoying the bodily motions of play, you are not playing well. Lose sight of the goal of enjoying your bodily experience, and you undercut the body's ability to execute its motions.

Competition can take us away from the pleasures of play precisely because it introduces status concerns. Status concerns, after all, make no direct reference to the workings of our bodies; they refer to how we are regarded by others. To compete well, we must integrate status concerns with our concerns for the pleasures of small motions.

Remember, if you will, the "Seven Circles of Concentration," from chapter three. The innermost circle is the body. Next comes the cue stick and ball, then the object ball, then the layout of the table. Then comes the competitive situation. As I said in chapter three, each outer circle provides information for the body. Competition introduces special concerns which have an impact on our bodily experience.

You might think (as most advisors seem to think) that the competitive situation provides no information for the body. You might think that a shot is a shot is a shot—that making a particular shot will require the same things from the body, no matter the conditions under which you shoot it. Hence, the ubiquitous whistling-past-the-graveyard advice to concentrate only on the shot in front of you. However, the competitive situation has immense impact on the body. Remember, from chapter five, that our unconscious appraisals generate emotions, which trigger bodily responses. Our appraisals always turn on our concerns. Whenever you compete, your status concerns enter into your appraisals, hence into your emotions, hence into your bodily responses. The competitive situation always has an impact on your body, whether or not you know (or like) that fact.

Remember, from the last two chapters, that our appraisals involve a projection of what we can expect—what sort of outcome we think we can effect. When you compete, your appraisals include not only an expectation of whether you can make the shot, but how the situation in front of you will affect your status. Precisely because competition introduces a whole range of concerns beyond making or missing the shot, competition engages your emotions in a different way than other forms of play. Every shot carries emotional significance for your status as a player. Competition, then, introduces special bodily challenges.

Remember that emotional engagement increases your motor controls and concentration, up to a point. For precisely as long as we believe that the shot before us presents an opportunity to enhance our status, the emotions generated by that appraisal help our play. However, as soon as we begin to doubt that we can effect a good outcome, one of two things happens. Either we panic or we give up.

Confidence, panic, or surrender: Those are the three basic emotional possibilities whenever we compete. Each of these affects the body differently. Your judgment of the competitive situation will affect your body. Remember that concentration requires that you know your current bodily state, the bodily processes necessary to complete the shot, and how to get from one to the other. When you compete, you must be aware of the impact of the competitive situation on your body, in order to get yourself to where you need to be. You have to know where you are, to know how to get where you need to go.

You might think that confidence requires no special physical effort; when you are confident, your body starts its motions from the best possible place. Generally, that is true. When you are confident, you only have to know how to go from a state of rest to the state of shooting this particular shot. Your intimate knowledge of the bodily processes required to make the shot is enough. However, confidence can become a problem, namely, when it leads us to forget that we still have to shoot. That is, when our expectation of establishing superior status is so strong that we act as if we were already there, we tend to become inattentive to the intricate processes of shooting. This tends to happen under two conditions: when we play a notably inferior opponent and when we have just made an amazing shot or run. We begin to think that we have already successfully concluded our quest for status. We think, "I'm the superior player. I have proven my status." Having satisfied our status concerns, we lose concern. More precisely, we have no motivation—no emotion—to prove what we believe we have already established. Thus, we become emotionally unengaged; our appraisal tells us, "The deed is done, mission accomplished—relax and enjoy it." We lose the motivation to pay attention to the first four, crucial circles of concentration, because we think we have nothing else to do.

How do you deal with this? Remember that a rational re-appraisal can always modify the emotions that have been generated spontaneously.

You have to counter your spontaneous self-satisfaction. You have to remind yourself that until the game is over, nothing has been proven. You have to call yourself back to attention. "Wait a minute. You're doing great, and that's great. But he could get a lucky break, or you could get a couple of bad rolls. He could get hot. Unless you stay engaged, you could go cold. Stay in this game—it isn't really over." Remind yourself of exactly what you still have to do. Keep your situation clearly before you. Otherwise, you will underestimate the significance of every shot, and your emotions will be ill-suited to each situation.

Panic occurs when you begin to anticipate the possibility of failure. Panic is the emotional state that occurs when we sense danger, know that we must escape it, but do not know how. In competition, the danger is loss of status. We tend to feel panic under two conditions: Something unexpected happens that puts us at risk, or something happens to which we do not know how to respond.

The first category, "the unexpected," includes missing a shot (or making a bad choice of shots) when we believed we had it in the bag (or believed we had thought through our choice carefully), or our opponent's suddenly beginning to play better than we thought he could. When we unexpectedly miss, we might think, "Maybe I'm not as good as I thought." When the opponent suddenly raises his game a notch, we might think, "Oh, my God—he's a lot better than I thought." In either case, uncertainty about our status ensues. If we do not resolve this uncertainty in a positive direction, we may panic.

The second category, a state of bewilderment, tends to occur when we face a situation in which we do not know what strategy to adopt or whether any shot within our repertoire will work. "Maybe I can't do this. Maybe this is the end of my hopes." Again, our status becomes uncertain, and failure to resolve the uncertainty positively may lead to panic.

When we panic, our bodies stop everything and prepare for anything. Our heart rates go up, our muscles tense, and we begin to scan the environment for clues what to do. We prepare for quick, extreme action at the first hint of what threatens us. So far as our evolution goes, that is a good thing: In a dangerous situation, where the menace is ill-defined, we need to leap to extreme action as soon as possible, if we are to survive. We do not have time for careful deliberations and well-crafted responses. Do it quick and do it big—that's the ticket to surviving unexpected or ill-defined dangers in the wild. For playing pool, this is not so good. Small motions require precision and exactitude. Neurologically and physiologically, we are not well-designed to exercise finesse under panic conditions. "The yips"—that bizarre phenomenon of the stick just wobbling around somewhere other than we intend—is the most dramatic illustration of this fact: We get them precisely from the effort to impose small motions, when the body is prepared for large ones. Less dramatically, we are likely to miscue or hit the cue ball someplace other than we intended, when we try to exercise small motions while our bodies want big actions.

When you begin to panic at the pool table, you have a lot of work to do. First and foremost, you must quell the "Do it quick and do it big" impulse. Some of our worst errors come out of this impulse. Attention narrows, and we look for the quick win—by playing some low-probability combination, maybe. We shoot too quickly, without attention to the precise bodily motions the shot requires. This is the time to use those relaxation techniques you have heard about. Breathe deep. Slow your heart rate. Check the tension in your shoulders, arms, and so forth; release it. Get yourself out of the "fight or flight" stance.

Paradoxically perhaps, aiming for pleasure becomes crucial in countering panic. Panic feels bad, if we feel it at all, because we are too tight. All muscles tense up, as we shift attention away from pleasure to survival. You must counter this destructive tension: "Wait a minute—I am not noticing my body. I am not feeling the pleasure of my motions. Let me get back in touch. Let me regain the good feeling of functioning well."

If your expectations and your sense of your ability harmonize with each other, you should rarely suffer panic. Certainly you will have anxiety—you will face difficult situations, in which your skills are challenged. But your emotions should fluctuate around a fairly steady, healthy baseline.

Remember that pool should always be pleasurable. When you become self-conscious, you forget about pleasure, you expect humiliation, and you feel bad. One way to know whether your mind set is sound is whether you enjoy the match. Whenever you lose the pleasure of play, you can be sure that you have lost concentration and rhythm. You have forgotten your body. You have become so consumed with status concerns that you have forgotten, for the moment, how to play.

Confidence, Pleasure, and Respect

Suppose that you enter your match in a sound frame of mind. You have an accurate sense of your ability, and you want to see who is the better player, at least on this occasion. You have no preconceived notions of the outcome, but you have a serious desire to win. Does that guarantee that you will remain psychologically sound throughout the game? Not at all. That is the mental baseline from which you should start; but the game itself presents immense challenges to sustaining an optimum mind set, as we have just seen. How do you keep your equilibrium through the vicissitudes of the match?

Pool advisors, borrowing from the terminology of sports psychology, like to talk about "mental toughness," as if keeping a sound mind required some sort of courage and fortitude. "Mental toughness" is a metaphor, not a scientifically meaningful term. Within sports psychology, it is a short-hand way of referring to some two dozen different dimensions of psychology. It is a slogan, a piece of rhetoric, not a validated concept. The metaphor derives from the ordinary notion of toughness: The ability to endure significant pain without losing the determination and ability to perform. Many sports do, in fact, require toughness; the metaphor is not out of place in those sports. Standing in front of someone who is trying to knock you unconscious requires toughness. Running through a pack of people bigger than you who want to grind you into the ground requires toughness. Forcing yourself to keep running a race when your lungs feel as though they are bursting and your legs weigh two tons each requires toughness.

Playing pool (like playing golf) does not, in fact, require toughness. Pool requires more finesse than fortitude, more quietude than courage. The metaphor of "toughness" is more misleading than helpful. Toughness calls for steeling yourself against your body's cries, ignoring the discomfort and agony you may feel. This is precisely the opposite of the attitude toward the body required by small motions. You should be exquisitely attuned to your body, not set against it. You should be enjoying its precision, not ignoring its signals. Pool, unlike many other sports, allows this, because there is no physical discomfort whatsoever involved in playing it well. Pool, unlike many other sports, demands this, because it is entirely about small motions.

In pool, unlike the sports in which the concept of mental toughness makes some amount of sense, we are never in danger of pain. We are rarely, in any significant sense, exhausted—and playing pool doesn't take much physical energy, anyway. We are never assaulted, unless we hustle the wrong people in the wrong room. We are in danger, at worst, of losing status.

Because the "toughness" metaphor conjures all the wrong connotations, we should banish it from pool psychology. Pool players tend toward too much macho posturing already, without our adding metaphors that make this seem like a psychological virtue.

A virtue that would make a far more enlightening metaphor for pool players would be "respect": respect for your skills, respect for your limitations, respect for the realities of the game. No one should ever aim to be "tough" at the pool table, simply because toughness is uncalled for. Rather, we should aim to be respectful.

When you suffer a threat to your status in competition, the biggest psychological danger is loss of confidence. But what is confidence, other than respect for your skills? Effective confidence—not the irrational, narcissistic fantasy that too many people mistake for confidence—is precisely a matter of knowing your tools and knowing what they are good for. What is that, but respect? Respect for your tools should not be shaken by fears about your status. The challenge, when faced with a threat to your status, is to remain truthful with yourself about what you know and what you can do. You do not have to endure pain; you have to address unfounded doubts about your ability. You do this by respecting what you know. You remind yourself of what, in fact, you can do.

Respecting the limitations of your tools and your skills is essential to doing a good job, in any field. A boxer who fails to respect the limits of his skills winds up on the canvas prematurely. A rock climber who ignores the limitations of his skills ends up dead. A pool player who ignores the limitations of his skills sits down, leaving the table open for his opponent. He tries shots and strategies he has no business trying, thus handing his opponent the opportunity to defeat him. He suffers no pain, but he suffers loss of status—essentially at his own hands. His failure to respect his limits insures his defeat.

The mental challenges of competition are all opportunities for and threats to our status. Thus, they are entirely about respect. "Respect," as a working metaphor, addresses directly the status concerns that lead us to compete at all. When we compete we are not trying to withstand anything—we are not letting others beat on us. Rather, we are seeking status—that is, respect. The only threats we face in competition are threats to the respect with which others view us.

Accordingly, it is helpful to think of the proper mind set for competition as a mind set of respect. We fear we will not be respected; we must, to deal with this, keep clear on exactly the respect we already know we have earned for ourselves. I do not mean by this anything like "self-esteem," much less that we should have some preconceived status accorded ourselves in our heads. As with confidence, this respect is not about the self at all. It is not even about victory. This is respect for the actual ability you have cultivated, its limits, and how those fit with the nature of the game. This is about what, in fact, you can do, not about whether you will win. Believing you will win is not necessarily smart; knowing exactly what skills you possess and what they are good for is bedrock good sense. Respecting that achievement is a positive attitude that those skills well deserve.

As the Zen types keep telling us, concern with the self defeats performance. As we have seen, self-consciousness destroys play. Yet competition is surely about status, which leads to concerns about ourselves. The resolution of this paradox is simple: Pool is not about yourself, after all; it is about your skills. Confidence is a matter of knowing your skills; a proper mind set for competition is to respect them. The status of your skills, not your worth as a person, is the issue when you compete.

In action, this means assessing truthfully and respectfully the quality of your skills. You do not denigrate them when you are anxious. You know what they are good for; you respect that. You trust them to do what they are capable of doing to bring you through. You do not exaggerate them when you play well; that is flattery, not respect. You do not lie to yourself, positively or negatively, ever, especially under pressure. Lies are disrespectful.

Thus, you keep your equilibrium by knowing what is true of your skills and respecting what they are good for. You use them with respect for their power. When threats to your status arrive, do not say, "I can win." Say, "I know which of my tools to use here, and I know what I can do with it." Then let yourself enjoy doing it.

When you are, in fact, performing well, relative to your ability, be satisfied with that. Competition establishes status. If, in fact, you are showing your true skills, whether you win or lose will be a fair indicator of your status. You compete to find out your status. Respect for your skills and their limits requires that you acknowledge honestly exactly the status you have earned.

The Romance of the Game

If you want to compete well, you must remember the pleasures of small motions. You must enjoy the bodily motions of rhythmic play. You must take pride in your skills.

Most of us play better in competition than practice, because our social status is on the line. We take greater care assembling our concentration. We make our wisest, most thoughtful shot choices. We plan our strategies as carefully as possible. As a result, the particular pleasures we will enjoy take place in service to winning. We do not forget pleasure in order to compete; we choose which things to enjoy by choosing which will help us win.

In fact, competing serves pleasure: Because we concentrate most carefully when we compete, because we choose our shots and strategies from within the most highly-developed parts of our repertoire, and because we play with the greatest possible attention to our bodies, competing is the most fun we can have at the table. Competing brings out the most precise and well-formed, and therefore most pleasurable, dimensions of our game.

Competing points up another great, usually unnoticed pleasure of the game: Whether you win or lose, you are part of something: a community of players. Competition establishes your ranking, at present, within that community. You can always aim to improve, and to increase your status. But competing, in and of itself, makes you part of the community of players, in a way that no other form of playing with pool can do. What an interesting community it is! In the pool hall, your skills and your demeanor toward other players are what matter. Social standing outside the pool hall is virtually irrelevant, so that truck drivers and stock brokers approach the table with no bias for or against either one. The history of our community embraces kings and thieves, gentlefolk and con men. Age hardly matters; except at the very top of the professional heap, a sixteen year old and a sixty year old may approach the table evenly matched. The pool community may be the most democratic, egalitarian community of sportsmen in the world.

You should not fail to enjoy your membership in the community of pool players. Belonging is as much a basic human need as play— probably more basic. Competition gives you entry into a community where status depends on skill and sportsmanship, and an adequate level of skill is open to all who care to pursue it.

Winning is not the main thing; the main thing is the pleasure of small motions. But competition crystalizes those pleasures, raising them to perfection—if you know how to allow it to do so. You should never lose sight of why you fell in love with the game. You should never let the pressures of status, the workaday worries of developing new skills, or the ups and downs of your game—the inevitable human variability of any activity—push from the center of your heart and mind why the game matters at all. It matters because it brings to your life the pleasures of precision, the joy of the exquisite power of small motions. It matters because it is beautiful. It matters because it is fun.

About the Author

Bob Fancher earned his Ph.D. at Vanderbilt University, then trained as a psychotherapist at Blanton-Peale Graduate Institute in New York City. He practiced psychotherapy in New York for fourteen years. His critically acclaimed book, *Cultures of Healing: Correcting the Image of American Mental Health Care*, has been used in classes at Columbia University, Princeton, Rutgers, and many other schools. His writings have appeared in *The Washington Post*, *Education Week*, and other publications—even *The Review of Metaphysics*! He writes the monthly column, "Dr. TBob, Pool Shrink," for *The American Cueist*. He now lives, writes, and plays pool in Austin, Texas.

References

For Further Reading

Until *Pleasures of Small Motions*, nothing has been written on the mental side of pool by anyone with even passing competence in psychology. For now, if you want to know more about the psychology of the game, you will have to turn straight to psychology books. Reasonably readable works on basic mental issues relevant to shooting pool include the following:

John Kremer and Deidre Scully. *Psychology in Sport*.
Philadelphia: Psychology Press. 1994.
> This is a scholarly, judicious overview of research and theory in sport psychology. Though the writing style is dry, the balanced perspective and careful analysis are priceless.

Stephen Pinker. *How the Mind Works*.
New York: Norton. 1997.
> A virtual encyclopedia of recent work on neuropsychology and cognitive neuroscience, written in a lively, wry style.

William H. Calvin. *The Cerebral Symphony*.
New York: Bantam. 1990.
> Beautifully written, enchanting and inspiring, this book gives a good introduction to the relations of conscious and unconscious processes, among other things.

Tor Norretranders. *The User Illusion.*
New York. Viking. 1998.
>The single best book I know on the limitations of conscious processing. Clearly written. The last chapter goes off the rails, giving the author's religious views, as he sees them deriving from his understanding of the mind, but prior to that, the book is soundly researched and argued.

Nico H. Frida. *The Emotions.*
New York: Cambridge University Press. 1986.
>The authoritative work on modern research into the emotions.

Albert Bandura. *Self-Efficacy.*
New York: W.H. Freeman. 1997.
>Bandura, one of the true giants of contemporary psychology, has done more research and theorizing on confidence—which he calls "self-efficacy," which means something like "the belief in one's ability to do things"—than anyone else. Though this is really a textbook, and Bandura has all the obtuse, jargon-loving habits of academic writers, the concepts are clear, and he does a good job of explaining how, in fact, confidence develops and functions.

Marvin Minsky. *The Society of Mind.*
New York: Simon and Schuster. 1985.
>The classic work on the modular, information-processing view of mind. Written explicitly for the lay audience, the book is a delight.

Antonio R. Dimasio. *Descartes' Error.*
New York: Putnam. 1994.
>Readable, clear account of how emotions, unconscious processes, and conscious thought interact, with special attention to the roles of the body in mental processes. Already a classic.